Cook it
step by step

A Dorling Kindersley Book

LONDON, NEW YORK,
MELBOURNE, MUNICH, and DELHI

Senior designer Sonia Moore
Senior editor Carrie Love
Design Clare Marshall
Additional design Jane Ewart, Gemma Fletcher,
Ria Holland, Jessica Bentall, Claire Patane,
and Charlotte Bull
Additional editing Nikki Sims
Photographer Will Heap
Additional photography Dave King
Illustrator Takashi Mifune
Category publisher Mary Ling
Home economists Aya Nishimura,
Paul Jackman, and Kate Blinman
Picture researchers Romaine Werblow
Proofreader Jennifer Lane
Production editor Raymond Williams
Production controller Seyhan Esen
Hand model Max Moore

First published in Great Britain in 2013
by Dorling Kindersley Limited, 80 Strand, London,
WC2R 0RL

Material used in this book was previously
published in:
Children's Cookbook (2004)
Children's Fun Healthy Cookbook (2007)
Grow It, Eat It (2008)
The Children's Baking Book (2009)
The Ultimate Children's Cookbook (2010)
Get Cooking! (2012)

Copyright © 2013 Dorling Kindersley Limited
A Penguin Company
2 4 6 8 10 9 7 5 3 1
187175 – 03/2013

A CIP catalogue record for this book is available from
the British Library

ISBN 978-1-40936-622-5

Printed and bound by South China Ltd in China

Discover more at
www.dk.com

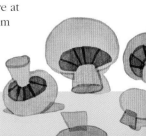

Contents

Introduction

Transforming a set of ingredients into something new is not only magical but is a great life skill. This book gives you ideas to try new breakfasts, snacks, main meals, and sweet treats. Whether you want to fry an egg, bake cookies, or concoct something more complicated, such as jambalaya, just follow the recipe's easy steps.

Getting started

1. Read a recipe all the way through before you start.
2. Wash your hands, put on an apron and tie back your hair.
3. Make sure you have all the ingredients and equipment before you begin a recipe.

Kitchen hygiene

When you're in the kitchen, follow these important rules to keep the germs in check.

• Always wash your hands before you start any recipe.

• Wash all fruit and vegetables.

• Use separate chopping boards for meat and vegetables.

• Keep your cooking area clean and have a cloth handy to mop up any spillages.

• Store raw and cooked food separately.

• Keep meat and fish in the fridge until you need them and always take care to cook them properly.

• Wash your hands after handling raw eggs or raw meat.

• Always check the use-by date on all ingredients.

• Discard leftover marinade that has been used to soak meat in.

Key to Symbols used in the recipes

How many people the dish serves, or how many portions it makes.

Preparation time, including chilling, freezing, and marinating.

Cooking time A few recipes, such as the salads, don't have this symbol.

Safety in the kitchen

Ask an adult to help when you see this symbol. Take extra care because hot ovens, hobs, or sharp implements, such as knives are involved.

Weights and measurements

Carefully weigh out the ingredients before you start a recipe. Use measuring spoons, weighing scales, and a measuring jug as necessary. Below are the full names for measurements and their abbreviations.

Metric measures

g = gram

ml = millilitre

Imperial measures

oz = ounce

lb = pound

fl oz = fluid ounce

Spoon measures

tsp = teaspoon

tbsp = tablespoon

HEALTHY EATING

You need to eat a balanced diet made up of a variety of different foods, so that you can grow, stay healthy, and have lots of energy for life.

Fruits and vegetables

Your body can get important vitamins and minerals, as well as fibre, from fruits and vegetables. Aim to eat about five different portions of these a day. It's useful to think of a portion as roughly equal to the amount you can hold in one hand – such as an apple, a small bunch of grapes, two broccoli florets, or a bowl of salad.

Starchy foods

Bread, cereals, rice, pasta, and potatoes are all starchy foods, also known as carbohydrates. These foods give you energy and should form a part of every meal – whether it's cereal for breakfast, a sandwich lunch, or a pasta dish for dinner. Many starchy foods come in whole-grain varieties, which are healthier for you as they contain more vitamins, minerals, and fibre, when compared with the refined white versions.

Protein

This type of food is made from amino acids, chemicals that work all over your body to keep you active and strong. We eat protein from both animal and plant sources – meat, fish, nuts and seeds, beans, and dairy produce. It's healthy to eat a variety of these.

Dairy produce

As well as being a source of protein, dairy produce provides valuable vitamins (vitamins A, B12, and D) and minerals (such as calcium). Dairy produce includes milk, yoghurt, cheese, butter, cream, crème fraiche, and cottage cheese. If you're not keen on dairy, then you can get these nutrients in other foods, such as soy milk, tofu, and baked beans.

Fats and sugars

Everyone needs fat for energy and for their bodies to work properly, it's just that it has to be the right type of fat. Fats also help you absorb vitamins and provide essential fatty acids, such as omega-3 and omega-6. Healthy fats (known as polyunsaturated or monounsaturated) are found in vegetable oils, such as sesame, sunflower, soy, and olive, as well as in nuts, seeds, avocados, and oily fish, such as mackerel and salmon. Avoid eating saturated and trans fats (mostly in processed foods).

Sugary foods and salt

Sugar gives you energy and it makes biscuits and cakes taste sweet. Eating too much sugar, though, can lead to mood swings, tooth decay, and obesity. Too much salt is linked with health problems. Avoid very salty snacks and adding too much salt to your cooking.

Equipment

You need to use the right equipment for each step. Most kitchens are equipped with the majority of these tools. Remember to be extra careful when using equipment that is sharp or uses electricity to power it. An adult should always supervise you while you're in the kitchen.

Peelers   Garlic crusher   Wooden Spoons   Whisk   Kitchen scissors   Basting brush   Large Spoon   Pizza cutter   Sharp knife   Table knife   Fork   Spoons

Grater   Baking trays   Loaf tin   Non-stick muffin tin

Pizza tray   Cutting boards   Cooling rack   Plastic container

Small bowls   Large bowl   Colander   Glass bowls   Milk pan   Wok

Food processor

Chopping board

Piping bag

Glass jar

Masher

Electric whisk

Food blender

Spatula

Plastic spatula

Ladle

Skewers

Sieve

Measuring Spoons

Egg cup

Slotted Spoon

Spaghetti claw

Ice cream scoop

Measuring jug

Pastry cutter

Ramekin

Lemon juicer

Cookie cutters

Sandwich cake tin

Glass jugs

Rolling pin

Square cake tin

Baking parchment

Foil

Oven dish

Ceramic flan dish

Lasagne dish

Metal flan dish

Cling film

Stock pot

Frying pan

Small casserole dish

Saucepan with lid

Griddle pan

Ways to cook

Some foods are best cooked at a low heat for a long time, while others respond best to a fast blast of heat. The different techniques shown below are used in different recipes to bring out the best flavours and textures of a dish.

Boil

With the heat turned up high, a liquid will bubble vigorously when boiling.

Simmer

With the heat on low, a mixture will bubble gently when simmering.

Fry

Drizzle some oil into a wide pan to fry food; it's also known as sautéing.

Stir-fry

On a high heat and using oil, stir-frying cooks fast and needs lots of stirring.

Grill

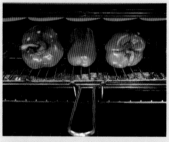

With the heat coming from above, you need to turn food during grilling.

Griddle

On a high heat, a griddle pan's ridges put smoky stripes on the food.

Bake

Cooking food in an oven is baking. Bread, biscuits, cakes, and pies are baked.

Roast

Cooking meat, fish, or vegetables in the oven is known as roasting.

Steam

Placing food above boiling water uses the steam to cook it.

Poach

Cooking in a simmering liquid, such as water or milk, is called poaching.

Deep-fry

Completely immersing food in hot oil is known as deep-frying.

BBQ

Food can be roasted or grilled on a BBQ using heat from charcoal.

Preparing ingredients

Before you start cooking you'll need to get all your ingredients ready. Depending on your recipe, you may have a lot of prep or very little to do.

Dice

To dice an onion, first slice it (while keeping it together) and then slice it at right angles to create small squares or dice. For a courgette, first cut into chunky sticks and then cut across these to make dice.

Chop

Claw Hold the food using a "claw" shape to keep fingers clear of the knife.

Bridge Form a bridge between thumb and finger and cut beneath the bridge.

Peel

Whatever you're peeling, hold the food in one hand and peel away from your body. Carrots are easily peeled from top to bottom but apples can be peeled in one beautiful spiral – with practice. And watch out for your fingers, peelers are sharp.

Grate

As the food passes over the grater's teeth, slithers are forced through.

Mash

Cooked root vegetables can be pushed through a masher until smooth.

Make breadcrumbs

Before

After

It's quickest done in a food processor. Tear pieces of dried-out bread into the bowl, pop the lid on, and whizz until crumbed. Or, you could grate chunks of the bread instead.

Other useful terms

- **Toast** to make a food, such as bread or nuts, crisp, hot, and brown (see page 81)
- **Puree** a thick pulp of vegetables or fruit blended till smooth in a liquidizer or pushed through a sieve (see page 31)
- **Marinate** to mix food with a combination of oil, wine, or vinegar with herbs or spices to add flavour (see page 76, 77, 88–89)

- **Blend** to mix together so you can't see any of the individual ingredients (see page 112)
- **Knock back** bash out the excess air when bread dough has risen, before letting it prove (see page 41)
- **Drizzle** pouring a little stream of liquid, such as olive oil, in tiny drops (see page 81)
- **Season** adding salt and pepper

- **Toss** mix some dry ingredients in some wet ingredients, such as lettuce leaves in salad dressing or pasta shapes in a sauce (see page 57)
- **Reduce to thicken** heating a sauce gently until some of its water is lost (as steam) and the amount of sauce becomes less (see page 83)
- **Baste** to coat food with meat juice, a marinade or butter, while cooking (see page 93)

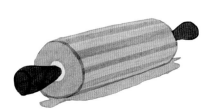

Ways to bake

To get cakes to rise, make light meringue, and perfect your pastry and biscuits, there are certain techniques in baking that you'll need to master. Once you know what's what you'll be a baking expert!

Sift

Shaking flour or icing sugar through a sieve gets rid of lumps and adds air.

Fold

1. Use a spatula to gently mix while keeping the air in the mixture.

2. Go around the edge of the bowl and then "cut" across, lifting as you go.

Beat

Make a smooth, airy mixture by working fast with a wooden spoon.

Separate an egg

1. Break the shell: tap the egg on the side of the bowl and open up.

2. Transfer the yolk from one shell to the other; put the yolk in another bowl.

Whisk egg whites

1. Mix in a lot of air into a mixture using an electric or a handheld whisk.

2. The mixture should be stiff; if you overwhisk the mixture will collapse.

Rub in

1. Many recipes mix fat (diced butter) and flour using this method.

2. Using your fingertips, pick up the mixture, break up the lumps, and let it fall.

3. Keep rubbing your thumb along your fingertips. To check you've got rid of all the lumps of butter, shake the bowl and any lumps will pop up to the surface.

Make a piping bag

1. Cut a square of greaseproof paper or baking parchment.
2. Fold the paper round on itself to form a cone with a pointy end. Tape in place.

3. Snip off the end of the cone for the icing or cream to come out: for a fine line use a tiny cut; cut higher up the cone for a chunky line.

Cream

1. When mixing butter and sugar together, use butter that's been left to soften at room temperature.
2. Cut the butter into pieces.

3. Using an electric whisk or a wooden spoon, beat the butter and sugar together until it's paler in colour, light, and fluffy.

Knead

1. Use the heel of your hand to push the bread dough away from you.

2. Fold the squashed end of dough over and turn the whole lot round.

3. Repeat the squashing, folding, and turning motions until the dough is silky soft and smooth. Now the dough is ready to prove (see page 40).

Roll out

On a floured surface, push down on a rolling pin to make a large flat piece.

Grease a tin

Use some baking paper to spread a thin layer of butter all over the tin.

Line a tin

1. Draw around your tin and add some extra for the paper to go up the sides.

2. Position the paper in the tin. Fold at the corners and snip off any extra bits.

BREAKFAST BITES

Ingredients

- 4 large eggs
- 240ml (8fl oz) milk
- ¼ tsp ground cinnamon
- 4 slices thick white bread, cut into triangles
- 2 tbsp sunflower oil
- 100g (3½oz) blueberries
- maple syrup, to serve

Equipment

- whisk
- mixing bowl
- shallow dish
- frying pan and spatula

Eggy bread

Popular around the world, this dish is eaten in Portugal at Christmas and in Spain and Brazil at Easter.

Serves 2   10 mins   10 mins

1

Crack the eggs into a mixing bowl. Add the milk and cinnamon and whisk together.

2

Pour the mixture into a shallow dish. Soak the bread (for about 30 seconds) in the mixture.

3

Heat half a tablespoon of the oil in a frying pan on a low heat. Carefully place two triangles in the pan.

4

Fry the triangles on both sides until they turn golden. Repeat steps 3 and 4 for the remaining bread triangles.

5

Serve the eggy bread warm, with blueberries and maple syrup or try it with butter and jam.

Four ways with eggs

Try these classic ways to cook an egg.

Boiled eggs

Boiled eggs are easy to make. How do you like your boiled egg? You can have it soft, medium, or hard-boiled.

Ingredients

This recipe is for 1 person. It takes 2 minutes to prepare and 4-8 minutes to cook.

• 1 egg

• 1 slice of toast, buttered

Method

• Fill a small saucepan with water and use a slotted spoon to lower one egg into it. Ask an adult to boil the water.

• When the water has boiled, lower the temperature and let it simmer. Follow these cooking times:

soft boiled 4 minutes
medium boiled 6 minutes
hard boiled 8 minutes

• Once cooked, use a slotted spoon to remove from the pan. Place in an egg cup and tap the top with the back of a teaspoon. Carefully slice off the top with a spoon. Serve with toast.

Scrambled eggs

Scrambled eggs are delicious on their own or as part of a cooked breakfast. You can add different ingredients, such as bacon.

Ingredients

This recipe is for 1 person. It takes 2 minutes to prepare and 8 minutes to cook.

• 1 slice of streaky bacon

• 1 tbsp milk

• 1 egg

• a small knob of butter

• dried basil, to serve

• 1 slice of toast, buttered

Method

• Ask an adult to grill the bacon. When it's cooked use a knife and fork to cut it up into small pieces.

• In a small glass bowl, use a hand whisk to mix together the milk and egg until creamy.

• Melt the butter in a small frying pan on a medium heat and add the egg and milk mixture. Stir often until the eggs are just cooked, but still creamy. Stir in the grilled bacon pieces with a wooden spoon.

• Sprinkle the dried basil over the eggs and serve on toast.

All sorts of shapes and sizes!

Most of the eggs we eat come from hens, but you can buy lots of different types. Go ahead and eggs-periment!

You can fit 24 hen eggs into one ostrich egg.

Quail

Duck

Hen

Gull

Goose

Ostrich

3

Poached egg

Poaching is a fun and satisfying way to cook an egg. You'll need an adult to help you as they can be tricky to make.

Ingredients

This recipe is for 1 person. It takes 1 minute to prepare and 1-2 minutes to cook.

· 1 egg, use a really fresh egg to get the best results

· 1 white muffin, halved, toasted and buttered, to serve

Method

● Fill a wide, shallow pan with water and ask an adult to heat it on a hob.

● When the water is simmering, use the handle of a slotted spoon to swirl the water round to make a whirlpool.

● Crack the egg into a small cup and tip it into the centre of the whirlpool.

● Use a slotted spoon to gently keep the water moving while the eggs cook, to give the cooked egg a round shape.

● When the egg has cooked, use a slotted spoon to remove it from the pan. Drain it on kitchen paper.

4

Fried egg

Fried eggs are quick to make and are a good way to have a filling breakfast. They are best served in a roll or on toast.

Ingredients

This recipe is for 1 person. It takes 1 minute to prepare and 2-4 minutes to cook.

· 1 tsp sunflower oil

· 1 egg

· 1 bread roll, halved and buttered

Method

● Ask an adult to heat the oil in a pan over a medium heat.

● Crack the egg into a bowl. If any of the shell falls into the bowl scoop it out using a spoon. Gently tip the egg into the frying pan.

● The egg needs to be fried for about two minutes on a medium heat. If you like your egg well-done, it needs to be cooked on both sides.

● Serve the fried egg on a buttered bread roll.

Ingredients

- 2 tbsp sunflower oil
- 6 tbsp golden syrup or runny honey
- 350g (12oz) rolled oats
- 115g (4oz) hazelnuts
- 60g (2oz) pumpkin seeds
- 115g (4oz) dried banana chips, broken into small pieces
- 115g (4oz) raisins
- milk or plain yoghurt to serve

Equipment

- large saucepan
- wooden spoon
- large bowl
- baking tray
- oven gloves
- airtight container to store cereal in afterwards

Fruity cereal

You need a hearty breakfast to keep you going through the morning. This delicious cereal will keep you filled up until snack time. You can try using dried cranberries instead of raisins.

Ask an adult to preheat the oven to 200°C (400°F/Gas 6). Heat the oil and golden syrup or honey in a saucepan over a low heat.

Pour the golden syrup and oil mixture into a large bowl with the oats, hazelnuts, and pumpkin seeds.

Place the mixture onto a baking tray, spread it out, and cook in the oven for 10 minutes or until the cereal turns a golden brown colour.

Let the oat mixture cool down on the tray and then tip it into a bowl. Add the dried banana chips and raisins to the mixture and stir well.

Serves 8   5 mins   20 mins

Storage

Store your cereal in an airtight container and have it for breakfast a few times over a couple of weeks. Don't keep it to yourself! Let your family and friends try it too.

5

Serve your cereal in a bowl with milk or a spoonful of plain yogurt. ⚠️

Fruit smoothies

Smoothies are great fun to make and drink. You can create lots of variations by using different fruit or by adding rolled oats to make your drink a bit thicker.

Here are three recipes...

Serves **3**   7 mins

Banana and mango smoothie

Ingredients

- 175ml (6fl oz) milk,
- 120ml (4fl oz) plain yogurt,
- 2 small bananas, sliced,
- 1 small mango, roughly chopped

Equipment

- chopping board, sharp knife, electric blender, glasses for smoothies

Method

- Follow the steps for the blueberry smoothie.

Peach and berry smoothie

Ingredients

- 120ml (4fl oz) milk,
- 120ml (4fl oz) plain yogurt,
- 2 peaches, sliced,
- 75g (2½ oz) raspberries,
- (2½ oz) strawberries, hulled,
- 1 tbsp rolled oats

Method

- Follow the steps for the blueberry smoothie.

Equipment

- chopping board, sharp knife, electric blender, glasses for smoothies

Blueberry, orange, and strawberry smoothie

Ingredients

- 120ml (4fl oz) smooth orange juice
- 120ml (4fl oz) milk
- 120ml (4fl oz) plain yogurt
- 150g (5½ oz) blueberries
- 150g (5½ oz) strawberries, hulled
- 3 tbsp rolled oats
- ½ tsp vanilla extract (optional)

Equipment

- chopping board, sharp knife, electric blender, glasses for smoothies

Method

- Put all the ingredients into a blender and run it on a medium to high speed until everything is well mixed and smooth.
- Pour the smoothie into three glasses and serve it to your family or friends.
- Drink straight away or you'll need to stir your smoothie as it will thicken and it can separate.

Sticky stuff

The sugar and golden syrup act like a glue in this recipe. They help the dry ingredients to stick together, making the muesli bars incredibly chewy and sticky!

Fruit bars

Cereal bars are perfect for breakfast or as a snack. Once you've mastered this recipe, experiment with other fruit and nuts.

Serves 12   15 mins   30 mins

1

Preheat the oven to 150°C (300°F/Gas 2). Grease your baking tin then line it with 2 sheets of baking paper.

2

Melt the butter, sugar, and golden syrup (or runny honey) in a saucepan over a low heat.

Ingredients

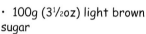

- 115g (4oz) unsalted butter
- 100g (3½oz) light brown sugar
- 115g (4oz) golden syrup or runny honey
- 300g (10oz) rolled oats
- 100g (3½oz) raisins
- 50g (1¾oz) mixed nuts, chopped

Equipment

- 30 x 23 x 4cm (12 x 9 x 1½in) baking tin
- baking paper
- wooden spoon
- saucepan

3

Place all the other ingredients in a large bowl and pour in the sugar mixture.

4

Spread the mixture evenly in the baking tin and, using a masher, press it down firmly so it sticks together. Bake for 20–30 minutes or until golden brown.

5

When the muesli bars are baked, leave them to cool for 5 minutes. Then, using a cloth to hold the tin, cut them into 12 squares. Remove them from the tin when fully cooled and firm.

LIGHT BITES

Tomato and couscous salad

Serves 4 · 30 mins

Salad makes a great light lunch or it can be eaten as an appetizer. This super salad is full of interesting ingredients and looks pretty on the plate. It's tasty, too!

Ingredients

- 4 large tomatoes
- 150ml (5fl oz) tomato juice
- 125g (4½oz) couscous
- 150ml (5fl oz) boiling water
- 50g (1¾oz) sultanas
- handful of basil leaves, chopped
- handful of flat-leaf parsley, torn (optional)

Equipment

- sharp knife
- chopping board
- teaspoon
- small glass bowl
- large glass bowl
- fork
- tablespoon

Slice the tops off the tomatoes and scoop out the insides. Put the seeds and flesh into a bowl with the tomato juice.

Pour the boiling water over the couscous, cover, and leave to stand for 10 minutes. Then, use a fork to fluff up the grains. Add the tomato mixture and stir.

Add the sultanas, basil, and parsley (if using), and mix. Taste, and season with ground black pepper as needed.

Spoon the mixture into the reserved tomato shells. Finally, serve with any leftover couscous mixture and garnish with some lettuce leaves.

Serves 4   30 mins

Tuna and bean salad

Salads are good for you as they help you to get your five portions of fruit and vegetables a day. This salad is full of interesting ingredients and is fun to make.

Ingredients

- 125g (4 ½ oz) frozen broad beans
- 400g can tuna in olive oil, drained
- 10 cherry tomatoes, halved
- handful of fresh chives, finely chopped
- ground black pepper
- 12 black olives, pitted
- 1 crisp lettuce such as Cos, leaves separated
- 2-3 spring onions, finely sliced

For the dressing

- 6 tbsp extra virgin olive oil
- 1 garlic clove, finely chopped
- 2 tbsp lemon juice
- 1-2 tsp Dijon mustard

Equipment

- large glass bowl
- colander
- screw-top jar
- 4 serving bowls

1

Soak the broad beans in hot water for five minutes, then use a colander to drain. Set aside.

2

To make the dressing, put all the ingredients in a screw-top jar, season with black pepper, cover with the lid, and shake!

3

4

Put the tuna, tomatoes, and half of the dressing in a bowl. Sprinkle in half of the chives and season with the pepper. Gently mix in the beans and olives.

Spoon the tuna mixture on top of the lettuce. Drizzle with the remaining dressing, and sprinkle over the spring onions and remaining chives.

24

Extras

If you don't like tuna then you can swap it for 400g of cooked ham slices or cooked chicken pieces, shredded. Also, you can try green olives instead of black olives.

Picnic salad

Ingredients

- 200g (7oz) couscous
- 300ml (½ pint) hot vegetable stock
- half a cucumber
- 1 medium pomegranate (or use 2 pre-peeled packets to save on time)

- grated zest and juice 1 lemon
- 2 tbsp olive oil
- 250g (9oz) cherry tomatoes, halved
- 1 small red onion, thinly sliced
- 200g (7oz) feta cheese, crumbled
- large bunch mint, freshly chopped

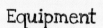

Equipment

- 3 bowls
- measuring jug
- fork
- chopping board
- knife
- teaspoon
- wooden spoon

This colourful salad is delicious and is a perfect picnic favourite. Swap the feta for one of your favourite cheeses, such as Cheddar, mozzarella, or Brie. And pop in some other ingredients, too – olives, peppers, and spring onions.

Place the couscous in a large bowl, pour over the hot stock and leave for 5 minutes until all the liquid has been absorbed. Allow to cool.

Halve the cucumber lengthways and scoop out the seeds with a teaspoon, then cut into pieces.

Cut the pomegranate in half, and hold one half over a bowl. Lightly tap the pomegranate with a wooden spoon, until the seeds fall into the bowl.

Stir the lemon juice, zest, and olive oil into the couscous. Add the tomatoes, cucumber, red onion, feta cheese, and mint, then stir in the pomegranate seeds.

Serves 4 15 mins 20 mins

Tomato soup

Soup is a comforting meal or snack
and makes an easy starter to a main meal. This soup
is wonderfully thick and creamy and is topped with
small pieces of toast, called croutons.

Serves 2-4 20 mins 35 mins

Ingredients

- 1 small onion
- 1 small carrot
- 4 tbsp olive oil
- 1 garlic clove, crushed
- 1 tbsp plain flour
- 400g (14oz) can chopped tomatoes
- 1 tbsp tomato purée
- 1 tsp fresh thyme leaves (optional)
- 450ml (15fl oz) vegetable stock
- a pinch of sugar
- a squeeze of lemon juice
- 2 thick slices of bread
- salt and pepper

Equipment

- sharp knife
- peeler
- chopping board
- medium saucepan
- wooden spatula
- bread knife
- non-stick baking tray
- oven gloves
- ladle
- blender

1

Peel and chop the onion and carrot. Ask an adult to preheat the oven to 220°C (425°F/Gas 7). Heat half the olive oil in the saucepan, over a medium heat.

2

Add the onion and carrot and cook for about 5 minutes to soften, stirring occasionally. Stir in the garlic and flour and cook the mixture for 1 minute.

3

Add the tomatoes, purée, thyme, stock, sugar, and lemon juice to the pan and bring to a boil. Reduce the heat and simmer for 20–25 minutes.

4

While the soup is cooking, use cookie cutters to cut out shapes for the croutons. Scatter the bread on the baking tray, drizzle over the remaining olive oil.

5

Use your hands to coat the bread in the oil and season. Bake for 8–10 minutes, until crisp and golden. Turn after about 4 minutes for even cooking.

6

Carefully ladle the hot soup into the blender. Taste the soup, season if necessary, and blend until smooth. Ladle into bowls and serve with the croutons on top.

Ingredients

- 1 kg (2¼lb) butternut squash
- 1 tbsp vegetable oil
- 1 onion (chopped)
- 600ml (1 pint) hot vegetable stock
- 2 tbsp honey

To serve
- French stick
- Gruyére or Swiss cheese
- freshly chopped parsley

Equipment

- tablespoon
- peeler
- baking tray
- wooden spoon
- food processor
- large saucepan

Butternut squash soup

This wholesome, warming soup is perfect for a cold day. It's made from roasted butternut squash, but you could also try it with pumpkin if you prefer.

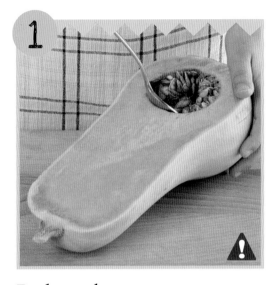

Preheat the oven to 200°C (400°F/Gas 6). Cut the butternut squash in half lengthwise, then use a spoon to scoop out the seeds and pith.

Cut into large chunks, then, using a peeler, remove the skin. Cut the chunks into 2.5cm (1in) cubes.

Place on a baking tray, season with salt and pepper, then drizzle over the oil. Roast for 20 minutes, then remove from the oven.

Add the onion and stir. Return to the oven and cook for a further 15 minutes.

Place the butternut squash and onion in a food processor with half of the stock and blend until smooth.

6

Place the puree in a saucepan with the remaining stock and honey. Simmer for 3 to 4 minutes. Serve with slices of toasted French stick, cheese, and parsley.

Serves 4   15 mins   39 mins

Basic bread

This recipe is easy and fun to make. Use the dough for a traditional loaf or for delicious rolls instead (you can make eight rolls with this dough).

Bread rolls

At Step 5, divide the dough into 8 balls, place on a greased baking sheet and flatten a bit. Cover with a damp tea towel and leave to rise for 30 minutes. Brush the tops with milk, and bake for 20 minutes.

Ingredients

- 1½ tsp active dried yeast
- 1 tsp caster sugar
- 360ml (12fl oz) lukewarm water
- 500g (1lb 2oz) strong white bread flour
- 2 tsp salt

Equipment

- a 1lb loaf tin
- sieve
- mixing bowl
- cling film
- cooling rack

Makes 1 loaf   1¾ hrs   30 mins

Lightly grease the loaf tin with butter, and set aside. Place the yeast, sugar and a little of the water in a small bowl, stir well and leave in a warm place for 10 minutes, until frothy.

Sift the flour and salt into a large mixing bowl. Make a well in the centre and pour in the yeast mixture and remaining water. Stir to form a dough. Knead the dough for 10 minutes on a floured surface.

Place the dough back in the bowl, cover with a damp tea towel and leave in a warm place for an hour. 'Knock back' the dough, by lightly punching it. (This knocks out the large air bubbles.)

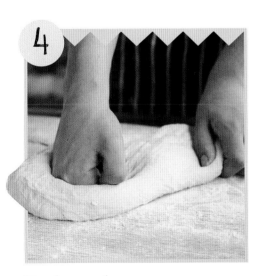

Preheat the oven to 220°C (425°F, Gas 7). Then knead the dough lightly on a floured surface.

It will DOUBLE in size!

Shape the dough into a rectangle and tuck the ends under to fit into the tin. Place in the tin. Cover with the damp tea towel and leave to rise in a warm place for a further 30 minutes.

Place the tin in the centre of the oven. Bake for 30 minutes, or until risen and golden. Turn out the loaf and tap the base – it should sound hollow. Place on a cooling rack.

Ingredients
- 350g (12oz) strong white bread flour
- ½ tsp salt
- 7g (¼oz) sachet fast-action dried yeast
- 175ml (6fl oz) warm water
- 4 tbsp olive oil
- 6 cherry tomatoes, halved
- 6 black olives, sliced
- coarse sea salt for sprinkling

Equipment
- sieve
- large mixing bowl
- large metal spoon
- baking tray
- clean damp tea towel
- rolling pin
- oven gloves

Italian bread

This dimpled bread is known as focaccia and can be flavoured with herbs, cheese, sundried tomato, or olives. It's so yummy, you'll keep coming back for more!

1

Lightly oil a baking tray to prevent the focaccia from sticking, and set aside. Sift the flour into a large mixing bowl, add the salt and stir in the yeast with a large metal spoon.

2

Make a well in the centre of the flour with the large metal spoon. Stir in the warm water and 3 tablespoons of olive oil until the mixture starts to come together to form a smooth dough.

3

Place on a floured surface surface. Knead for 10 minutes until smooth and elastic. Place in a bowl, cover with a tea towel and leave to rise in a warm place for 1 hour.

4

'Knock back' the dough to remove the large air bubbles, then place on a floured surface. Roll out to a rectangle (that fits on the tray) about 1cm (⅜in) thick.

5

Place the rolled-out dough on the oiled baking tray and cover with a clean damp tea towel. Leave the dough to rise in a warm place for 30 minutes.

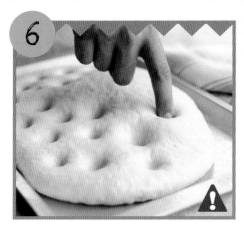

6

Preheat the oven to 200°C (400°F/Gas 6). Using your fingertips, make dimples all over the surface of the risen dough.

7

Drizzle the remaining olive oil over the dough and place rosemary in a third of the dimples, fill another third with the tomatoes and olives.

8

Sprinkle over the sea salt concentrating on the empty dimples. Bake on the middle shelf for 20–25 minutes until risen and golden. Delicious eaten warm.

Serves 6   2 hrs   25 mins

Sunflower loaves

Serves 4   140 mins   35 mins

Fill your kitchen with the homely smell of bread-making. Sunflower seeds are great to nibble on, too, while your bread is baking.

Ingredients

- 250g (9oz) strong white bread flour
- 150g (6½oz) wholemeal flour
- 1 tsp salt
- 1 tsp sugar
- 1 sachet 7g (¼oz) fast-action yeast

- 250ml (8fl oz) warm water
- 2 tbsp extra virgin olive oil, plus extra for oiling pots
- 100g (4½oz) sunflower seeds
- a little milk

Equipment

- 4 terracotta flower pots, 11 x 10cm (5 x 4in)
- measuring jug
- mixing bowl
- baking tray
- plastic bag
- pastry brush
- wooden spoon

Scrub the pots with clean water. Ask an adult to preheat the oven to 200°C (400°F/Gas 6). Oil the pots inside and out and bake for 35–40 minutes. Let them cool. Repeat this process twice more.

Put the flour, salt, sugar, and yeast into a large bowl. Make a well in the centre and pour in the water and olive oil. Mix to make a soft, but firm dough.

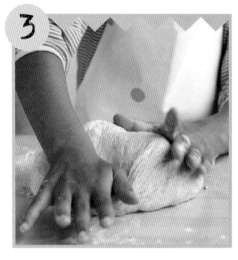

Turn the dough out onto a lightly dusted work surface and knead well for at least 10 minutes (use a timer). Ask an adult to take a turn if your arms get tired.

Make a dip in the dough and add three-quarters of the sunflower seeds. Knead them into the dough so that they're evenly spread.

Divide the dough into four pieces and place one ball into each flower pot. Cover the pots with a plastic bag and leave until the dough has doubled in size.

Brush the tops of the risen loaves with a little milk. Sprinkle over the remaining sunflower seeds and bake for 35–40 minutes or until golden. Cool in the pots.

Cornbread

This cornbread recipe is really simple to make and the sweetcorn and spring onions give it an unusual texture.

Ingredients

- 125g (4½oz) plain flour
- 125g (4½oz) cornmeal or polenta
- 1 tbsp baking powder
- 1 tsp salt
- 5 spring onions, thinly chopped, optional
- 150g (5½oz) tinned sweetcorn
- 2 medium eggs
- 284ml carton buttermilk or natural yogurt
- 100ml (3½fl oz) milk
- 50g (1¾ oz) butter, melted and cooled

Equipment

- 20cm (8") square cake tin or a 20cm (8") ceramic pie dish, ceramic or metal
- pastry brush
- large mixing bowl
- wooden spoon
- measuring jug
- whisk
- oven gloves
- sharp knife

Grease a 20cm (8") square cake tin or a round 20cm (8") ceramic pie dish. The recipe works in either a tin or dish. Preheat the oven to 200°C (400°F/Gas 6).

In a large mixing bowl, place the flour, cornmeal or polenta, baking powder, salt, chopped spring onions, and sweetcorn. Mix together thoroughly with a wooden spoon and set aside.

In a measuring jug, whisk together the eggs, buttermilk (or yogurt), milk, and melted butter with a small hand whisk until they are thoroughly combined and frothy.

Pour the egg and milk mixture into the flour mixture in the large mixing bowl. Stir with a wooden spoon to combine all the ingredients thoroughly.

5

Pour the mixture into the prepared tin. Bake for 25–30 minutes until golden brown, and beginning to pull away from the sides of the tin. Allow to cool in the tin before cutting into wedges.

Pizza dough

Pizza is a popular meal to eat for lunch or dinner. It's easy to learn how to make the dough for the base. This recipe makes enough dough for four pizzas.

Ingredients

- 500g (1lb 2oz) "00" or strong white flour
- 7g sachet of fast-action dried yeast
- a pinch of salt
- 200ml (7fl oz) warm water
- 4 tbsp olive oil

Equipment

- sieve
- large glass bowl
- wooden spoon
- cling film
- baking tray or tin
- rolling pin

makes 4 pizzas   1 hr

1

Sift the flour into a bowl and add the yeast and salt. Make a well in the centre, then slowly add the warm water.

2

Mix with a wooden spoon until it comes together and then add the olive oil and continue to mix until it forms a soft dough.

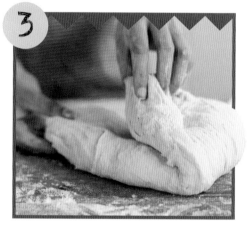

3

Knead firmly using the heel of your hand, folding the dough over as you go. Do this until the dough becomes soft and spongy.

4

Put the dough in a bowl, cover with cling film, and leave in a warm place for 30–40 minutes or until the dough has doubled in size.

5

Put the dough on a floured surface, and knead with your knuckles to knock out the air. Fold the dough over and knead again.

It will become elastic and stretchy

40

6 **Divide the dough** into four balls. Using a rolling pin, roll a ball out on a floured surface until it's about a centimeter (½ in) thick. Place on a pizza tray or in a metal tin. You can try out different toppings.

Below, the dough is topped with 3 tbsp tomato puree, 3 tomatoes (sliced), and 150g (5½oz) mozarella (torn into pieces), and fresh basil leaves.

Bake for 15–20 minutes or until the crust is golden and the cheese is bubbling.

Four ways with pizzas

Try out these classic and new pizzas.

(1)

Tiny toms pizza

This is a classic combination of ingredients and flavours. Restaurants that serve pizza would have this at the top of their list.

Ingredients

- pizza dough ball (from the recipe on pages 40–41)
- 2-3 tbsp tomato puree or passata
- mozzarella ball
- 1 punnet of tiny tomatoes
- fresh basil leaves, to serve

Method

- Roll out your pizza dough on a floured surface into a circle that will fit your pizza tray.
- Spread the tomato puree over the pizza using the back of a spoon.
- Carefully cut the mozzarella ball into slices.
- Place the mozzarella slices onto the pizza (slightly overlapping) and scatter the tiny tomatoes on the cheese.
- Cook the pizza in a preheated oven, 180°C (350°F/ Gas 4) for 20 minutes.
- Garnish with a handful of fresh basil leaves, torn.

(2)

Hawaiian bites

These are a fun take on ham and pineapple pizza. They'll be snapped up quickly so make sure you try one before they all go!

Ingredients

- pizza dough ball (from the recipe on pages 40–41)
- 2-3 tbsp tomato puree or passata
- 212g can of pineapple pieces, drained
- 60g (2½oz) ham, cut into strips
- 150g (5½oz) grated mozzarella cheese

Method

- On a floured surface, divide your pizza dough into 12 small balls. Flatten the balls so they form small circles that are about 8cm (3in) in diameter.
- Spread the tomato puree over the dough circles using the back of a spoon.
- Place a couple of pineapple pieces and a few strips of ham onto each pizza.
- Sprinkle a little bit of grated mozzarella cheese over each pizza bite.
- Cook the pizzas in a preheated oven, 180°C (350°F/ Gas 4) for 15 minutes.

anchovies

baby spinach leaves

sliced sweet peppers

pineapple

olives

chilli peppers

pepperoni

cherry tomatoes

(3)

(4)

Mushroom madness

If you're a pizza fan then this option will be right up your street. The mushrooms and mozzarella will melt in your mouth.

Ingredients

- 1 tbsp olive oil

- 125g (4¹/₂oz) mushrooms, sliced

- pizza dough ball (from the recipe on pages 40–41)

- 2-3 tbsp tomato puree or passata

- mozzarella ball

Method

● Gently heat the oil in a frying pan and fry the mushrooms for 2 minutes.

● Roll out your pizza dough on a floured surface into a circle that will fit your pizza tray. Roll the dough as thinly as you can.

● Spread the tomato sauce over the pizza using the back of a spoon.

● Cut the mozzarella ball into thin slices.

● Place the mozzarella and mushrooms onto the pizza.

● Cook the pizza in a preheated oven, 180°C (350°F/ Gas 4) for 20 minutes.

Pizza-pops

These fun lollipop-style pizzas are great for a party or picnic. The combination of peppers and tomatoes is delicious.

Ingredients

- pizza dough (from the recipe on 40-41)

- 2-3 tbsp tomato puree or passata

- 150g (5¹/₂oz) grated mozzarella cheese

- half a yellow pepper, sliced

- 6 red cherry tomatoes, halved

- 6 yellow cherry tomatoes, halved

Special equipment

- white oven-proof sticks

Method

● Divide your pizza dough into 12 small balls. Flatten the balls so they form small circles that are approximately 8 cm (3 in) in diameter. Insert a stick into each uncooked dough circle.

● Spread the tomato sauce over the circles using the back of a spoon.

● Decorate with grated mozzarella, peppers, and tomatoes.

● Cook the pizzas in a preheated oven, 180°C (350°F/ Gas 4) for 15 minutes.

43

Club sandwich

This triple-decker deluxe lunch uses ham, chicken, and cheese. But you can choose any ingredients you like to build your own stackable sandwich.

Serves 4   10 mins

Ingredients

- 6 slices white bread (you could use the bread from the Basic bread recipe, page 32)
- 4 tbsp mayonnaise
- 1 tbsp lemon juice

- 50g (1¾oz) iceberg lettuce, shredded
- 2 slices ham
- 2 slices Swiss or Cheddar cheese

- 1 tomato, sliced
- 50g (1¾oz) cooked chicken breast, shredded

Equipment

- bread knife
- cutting board
- mixing bowl
- metal spoon
- toothpicks

1

Lightly toast the bread on both sides in a toaster or under a preheated moderate grill (ask an adult to help). Cut off the crusts.

2

In a small bowl, mix together the mayonnaise and lemon juice. Season to taste and then stir in the shredded lettuce.

3

Spread 2 slices of the white toast with half of the lettuce and mayonnaise mixture.

4

Place a slice of ham, then a slice of cheese on top of each. Top with another slice and spread with the remaining lettuce and mayo.

5

Add some slices of tomato and the chicken. Top with the remaining toast.

6

Cut each sandwich into 4 triangles and secure each one with a toothpick.

Pitta pockets

Tofu is a versatile and nutritious ingredient. The sauce used in this recipe gives the tofu a yummy barbecue taste as well as an appealing glow.

Ingredients

- 250g (9oz) firm tofu
- a little olive oil
- 3 Cos lettuce leaves, shredded
- 2 spring onions, peeled and cut into long strips
- a handful of alfalfa sprouts, optional
- 4 wholemeal pitta bread, warmed in a toaster or warm oven

For the marinade

- 2 tbsp sweet chilli sauce
- 2 tbsp tomato ketchup
- 2 tbsp soy sauce
- ½ tsp ground cumin

Equipment

- small sharp knife
- chopping board
- kitchen towel
- dessert spoon
- shallow dish
- griddle pan
- spatula or tongs

1

In a shallow dish, mix together all the ingredients for the marinade, set aside. Pat the tofu dry with a kitchen towel and cut it into 8 long slices.

2

Put the tofu into the dish with the marinade. Spoon the marinade over the tofu until it is well coated. Leave the tofu to marinate for at least 1 hour.

3

Brush the griddle pan with a generous amount of olive oil and then put it on a high heat. Carefully put 4 of the tofu slices into the hot pan.

4

Cook the tofu for 4 minutes on each side, or until golden. As you cook, spoon over more of the marinade. Griddle the rest of the tofu in the same way.

5

Serves 4 **80 mins** **16 mins**

Carefully slice along the edge of the pitta bread. Divide the lettuce, spring onions, and alfalfa sprouts between the pitta bread and then add 2 pieces of tofu.

Variation

Strips of chicken, pork, turkey, or beef or even a medley of vegetables such as pepper, courgette, and onion make a great alternative to the tofu.

47

Ingredients

- 1 cucumber
- 2 celery sticks
- 1 red pepper, deseeded
- 1 yellow pepper, deseeded
- 2 carrots
- 4 baby gem lettuce leaves
- 8 cherry tomatoes
- 4 broccoli florets

Sour cream and chive dip

- 8 tbsp sour cream
- 3 tbsp fresh chives, chopped
- 2 tsp lemon juice

Yogurt and mint dip

- 250g (9oz) natural yogurt
- ½ cucumber, grated
- 2 tsp dried mint

Equipment

- sharp knife
- chopping board
- 8 colourful cups and tray/platter (to serve vegetables in)
- 2 small glass bowls
- 2 tablespoons

Vegetable platter

This healthy and colourful snack works well for any occasion or as a side dish to accompany a light meal.

Carefully slice the cucumber, celery sticks, peppers, and carrots into thin strips.

Place the vegetable sticks lettuce leaves, cherry tomatoes, and broccoli florets into colourful cups on a tray and set aside.

Mix the sour cream, chives, and lemon juice in a small glass bowl. Pour into a colourful cup to serve.

In another small glass bowl mix the natural yogurt, grated cucumber, and dried mint together. Taste and season with salt and pepper. Serve in a colourful cup.

Serves 4   20 mins

Alternatives

There are plenty of other vegetables and dips you can try out for a vegetable platter. So, why not try out green beans and sugar snap peas and a guacamole dip?

Four ways with starters

Try out these these tasty bruschettas.

1

Tiny tomatoes

This is a delicious combination of ingredients and flavours. The mozzarella melts in your mouth and the tomatoes are so juicy.

Ingredients

This recipe is for 4 people. It takes 5 minutes to prepare and 2 minutes to cook.

· ciabatta loaf, sliced

· 125g (4½oz) mini mozzarella balls

· 1 punnet of tiny tomatoes

· 8 fresh basil leaves

Method

• Toast the slices of ciabatta until golden under a grill. You may have 1 or 2 slices left over at the end.

• Carefully slice the tiny tomatoes in half.

• Place the mozzarella balls and tiny tomatoes on the toasted slices of ciabatta.

• Scatter a couple of basil leaves on each slice of ciabatta.

• Serve as individual portions or on a large tray.

2

Criss-cross ham

The salty ham and melted cheese make this bruschetta a yummy starter. It will be a real winner with your friends or family.

Ingredients

This recipe is for 4 people. It takes 5 minutes to prepare and 4 minutes to cook.

· ciabatta loaf, sliced

· 125g (4½oz) ham

· 170g (6oz) Cheddar cheese

Method

• Toast the slices of ciabatta until golden under a grill. You may have 1 or 2 slices left over at the end.

• Cut the ham into thin strips and the cheese into generous slices.

• Place the cheese slices onto the ciabatta and then add the ham in a criss-cross pattern.

• Grill the bruschettas for 2 minutes or until the cheese begins to bubble. Be careful not to let the ham get overcooked.

• Serve as individual portions or on a large tray.

Make your own

Bruschetta is an Italian starter that traditionally consists of toasted bread with garlic, olive oil, salt and pepper. You can also try out these ingredients.

cheese

baby spinach leaves

red pepper

basil

roasted vegtables

salami

tomatoes

3

4

Carrot butter

The moist carrots and rich butter make this bruschetta a real favourite. You can keep any leftover mixture in the fridge for a few days.

Ingredients

This recipe is for 4 people. It takes 1 hour to prepare and 2 minutes to cook.

· ciabatta loaf, sliced

· 1 onion, finely chopped

· 4 carrots, finely grated

· 1 tsp tomato puree

· 1 tsp dried oregano

· 225g (8oz) butter

Method

• On a medium heat, fry the onions in a teaspoon of oil.

• Blend the onion, carrots, tomato puree, oregano and butter in a food processor.

• Place the mixture in a bowl, cover, and refrigerate the mixture for 1 hour.

• Toast the slices of ciabatta until golden under a grill. You may have 1 or 2 slices left over.

• Generously spread the carrot butter onto the slices of toasted ciabatta and serve as individual portions or on a large platter.

• Garnish with fresh coriander leaves if desired.

Cheese and cucumber

These bright and fun bruschettas are great for a party. Use the remaining cucumber to make sticks to accompany the dish.

Ingredients

This recipe is for 4 people. It takes 5 minutes to prepare and 4 minutes to cook.

· ciabatta loaf, sliced

· 200g (7oz) cream cheese

· 1 cucumber

Method

• Toast the slices of ciabatta until golden under a grill. You may have 1 or 2 slices left over at the end.

• Spread the cheese evenly over the bruschettas.

• Use a knife carefully to peel a cucumber and use cookie cutters to make decorative shapes out of the peel and flesh of the cucumber.

• Place the shapes on the bruschettas and serve on individual plates or on a large platter.

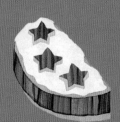

MAIN MEALS

Serve in small casserole dishes

Lamb hotpot

Serves 6   25 mins   20 mins

This hotpot is a hearty main meal that will fill you up. The lamb and tomatoes make it juicy and the chickpeas add texture. Serve it with crusty bread rolls.

1

Put the lamb, flour, and paprika into a mixing bowl and combine well so that the lamb is coated.

2

Heat the oil in a large pan over a medium heat, add the onions, and cook, stirring often, for 5 minutes. Add the lamb and cook until browned.

3

Stir in the garlic and chickpeas, and cook for one minute. Add the tomatoes, bring to the boil, then simmer for 15 minutes.

4

Season well with ground black pepper, stir in the spinach, and cook for 3 minutes.

Ingredients

- 175g (6oz) lean lamb, leg or fillet, cut into 2cm (3/4in) diced
- 1/2 tbsp plain flour
- 1/4 tsp paprika
- 1 1/2 tbsp olive oil
- 1/2 large red onion, sliced
- 2 garlic cloves, chopped
- 1/2 400g can chickpeas, drained and rinsed
- 400g can chopped tomatoes
- 125g (4 1/2 oz) baby leaf spinach
- crusty bread rolls, to serve, optional

Equipment

- large glass bowl
- large pan
- wooden spoon
- 6 bowls or individual casserole dishes to serve the hotpot in

Ingredients

- 2 eating apples
- 2 tbsp olive oil
- 6-8 sausages, turkey, pork, beef, or vegetarian
- 1 onion, chopped
- 1 carrot, diced
- 2 cloves garlic, finely chopped

- 110g (4oz) lean back bacon, cut into bite-sized pieces, optional
- 1 tsp mixed herbs
- 400g (14oz) tinned borlotti or pinto beans, drained and rinsed
- 4 tbsp tinned chopped tomatoes
- 1 tbsp tomato puree

- salt and pepper
- 400ml (14fl oz) chicken or vegetable stock

Equipment

- vegetable peeler
- small sharp knife
- chopping board

- large ovenproof pan with lid or large saucepan and large casserole dish with lid
- oven gloves
- wooden spoon
- jug
- tongs

1

Carefully remove the skin of the apples using a vegetable peeler. Quarter them and remove the core. Cut the apples into bite-sized pieces and set aside.

2

Preheat the oven to 200°C (400°F/Gas 6). Heat the oil in a large saucepan or ovenproof pan and cook the sausages for 5 minutes, or until browned all over.

3

Remove the sausages from the pan and set aside. Put the onion and carrot into the pan and fry over a medium heat for 5 minutes, stirring frequently.

4

Next, add the garlic, bacon, and herbs, stir well, and cook for 6 minutes. (Transfer to a large casserole dish if you aren't using an ovenproof pan.)

5

Add the beans, tomatoes, tomato purée, apples, and sausages and stir. Pour in the stock and bring to the boil.

6

Cover with a lid and place in the preheated oven. Cook for 25 minutes. The sauce should reduce and thicken and the apples will become tender.

Sausage hotpot

Fruit gives this savoury dish a natural sweetness and an extra vitamin boost. You can serve this winter warmer with fluffy mash and steamed green vegetables.

Serves 4   20 mins   45 mins

7 **Take care** when removing the casserole dish from the oven as the hotpot will be very hot. Season with salt and pepper.

Beef pasta

This pasta dish is an easy main meal to make for you and your family. The combination of beef and mushrooms is super-tasty.

Ingredients

- 1 small onion, finely chopped
- $^1/_2$ tbsp olive oil
- ground black pepper
- 250g (9oz) good-quality beef mince
- 100g (3$^1/_2$oz) mushrooms, finely chopped
- pinch of dried oregano
- 1 garlic clove, finely chopped
- 400g can of chopped tomatoes
- 1 tbsp tomato puree
- 1 tsp green pesto
- 200g (7oz) tortiglioni pasta

Equipment

- frying pan
- wooden spoon
- saucepan
- colander

1

Cook the onion in the oil over a low heat. Season with pepper, then stir in the beef and cook, stirring, until no longer pink.

2

Add the mushrooms, oregano, garlic, tomatoes, and tomato puree and stir well. Simmer for 10 minutes, then stir in the pesto.

3

Meanwhile, ask an adult to cook the pasta in a pan of boiling water. Using a colander, drain the pasta (over a bowl or sink), toss with the meat sauce, and serve.

Fresh tomato pasta

You don't need to cook the sauce for this pasta dish. It's deliciously fresh and fast to make. The classic flavours of tomato and basil are perfect together.

1

Put the tomatoes, garlic, basil, and olive oil in a large bowl and season with black pepper. Stir the mixture together using a wooden spoon.

2

Ask an adult, to cook the pasta in a saucepan of boiling water. Using a colander, drain the pasta well, then toss with the tomato sauce and serve.

Serves 4   5 mins   10 mins

Ingredients

- 2 large red onions
- 2 large carrots
- 2 large courgettes
- 2 red peppers, de-seeded
- 1 medium aubergine
- 2 yellow peppers, de-seeded
- 4 tbsp olive oil
- 2 tsp chopped fresh rosemary
- 2 garlic cloves, crushed
- 400g can chopped tomatoes
- 1 tbsp tomato puree
- 9 dried lasagne sheets

For the sauce

- 60g (2oz) unsalted butter
- 30g (1oz) plain flour
- 500ml (16fl oz) warm milk
- 125g (4½oz) Parmesan cheese, grated

Equipment

- chopping board
- sharp knife
- roasting tin
- oven gloves
- large saucepan
- wooden spoon
- small saucepan
- whisk
- lasagne dish (approx. 25 x 18cm and 5cm deep (10 x 7in and 2in deep)
- serving spoon

Vegetable lasagne

A crowd-pleasing dish that's a meal in its own right, this lasagne makes a welcome change from the meat-based one. Why not experiment with other flavours?

Ask an adult to preheat the oven to 220°C (425°F/Gas 7). Cut the onions into wedges and then chop all the other vegetables into chunks.

In the roasting tin, mix the oil, rosemary, and garlic with the vegetables and season. Roast for 35 minutes, shaking the tin occasionally.

Gently warm through the tomatoes and tomato puree in a large saucepan. Take the pan off the heat and carefully stir in the roasted vegetables.

On a low heat, melt the butter in a pan. Stir in the flour. Cook for 1 min. Whisk in the milk. Stir until thickened. Add half the cheese and season.

5

Turn down the oven to 190°C (375°F/Gas 5). Spoon a third of the vegetables into the the dish and top with 3 lasagne sheets.

6

Add another third of the vegetables, top with another layer of lasagne, pour over half the sauce, and then the remaining vegetables.

7

Finally lay on the remaining lasagne sheets and drizzle over the sauce. Sprinkle the cheese over the top and bake for 35 minutes or until golden and bubbling.

Serves 6   50 mins   1 hr 15 mins

Variations

Add variety to this light meal by serving it with a mixture of steamed vegetables or a fresh garden salad with leaves, cherry tomatoes, and cucumber slices.

Rice balls

This dish works well as a light main meal or as a filling starter. The soft rice and melted mozzarella are tasty and have a great texture.

Ingredients

- 225g (8oz) cold cooked Arborio or other risotto rice
- ground black pepper
- 1 large ball of buffalo mozzarella, cut into cubes
- 1 egg, beaten
- 2 slices of toast, for breadcrumbs
- olive oil, for deep frying
- salsa dip, to serve
- salad, to serve

Equipment

- large glass bowl
- dinner plate
- spoon
- small bowl
- large dish
- large saucepan
- sieve
- kitchen paper

1

Generously season the rice with black pepper and stir with a spoon to make sure the pepper is well mixed. Roll the rice into 12 evenly-sized balls.

2

Make a hole in each rice ball. Push a cube of mozzarella cheese into the centre of each ball, then cover so that the cheese is enclosed.

3

Completely coat the balls

Roll each ball in the egg and then roll in the breadcrumbs (bread or toast that's been turned into crumbs in a food processor - see page 9 for how to make breadcrumbs).

4

Ask an adult to deep fry the balls in olive oil over a medium heat for 2–3 minutes or until golden. Place the balls on kitchen paper to soak drain some oil. Serve the balls with salad and salsa.

Jambalaya

This is a colourful Creole or Cajun rice dish from Louisiana in the USA. It's simple to make because all the ingredients are cooked in the same pot.

Serves 4   20 mins   50 mins

Ingredients

- 250g (9oz) brown rice
- 1 large onion, chopped
- 3 skinless chicken breasts
- 200g (7oz) smoked ham
- 2 tbsp olive oil
- 2 large cloves garlic, chopped
- 1 red pepper, deseeded and cut into bite-sized pieces
- 1 green chilli, deseeded and finely chopped (optional)
- 1 tsp paprika
- 1 tsp dried thyme
- 700ml (1¼ pints) warm chicken or vegetable stock
- 3 tbsp tinned chopped tomatoes
- 50g (1¾oz) peas

Equipment

- sieve
- small sharp knife
- chopping board
- large saucepan with lid
- wooden spoon

1

Put the rice in a sieve and rinse it under cold water until the water runs clear. Washing the rice before cooking stops the grains of rice sticking together.

2

Chop the onion into small pieces and set aside. Carefully cut the chicken and ham into bite-sized pieces. Heat the oil in the large saucepan.

3

Fry the chicken and onion for 8 minutes over a medium heat until the chicken is golden all over. Stir frequently so it doesn't stick to the pan.

4

Add the ham, garlic, red pepper, and chilli, and cook for 2 mins. Add the paprika, thyme, rice, stock, and tomatoes. Stir and bring to the boil.

5

Reduce the heat to low, cover the pan and simmer for 35 mins or until the rice is cooked and the water is absorbed. Season the rice and stir before serving.

Variations

The recipe can be easily adapted for vegetarians by replacing the chicken and ham with extra vegetables, meat-free sausages, beans, or tofu.

Potato salad

This simple potato salad is a classic. It substitutes traditional mayonnaise for a lighter creamy sauce, flavoured with fresh chives.

Ingredients

- 500g (1lb 2oz) baby new potatoes
- 3 tbsp reduced fat crème fraîche
- 3 tbsp low-fat yogurt
- 2 tbsp freshly chopped chives

Equipment

- knife
- cutting board
- saucepan
- 2 mixing bowls
- metal spoon

1

Give the potatoes a thorough clean. Make sure there's no mud left on them. Cut any larger potatoes in half.

2

Cook in a pan of lightly salted boiling water for 12 to 15 minutes. Drain and allow to cool. Place in a mixing bowl.

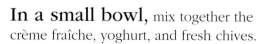

3

In a small bowl, mix together the crème fraîche, yoghurt, and fresh chives.

4

Gently stir the chive mixture into the potatoes. Season to taste. Keep refrigerated until ready to serve.

Serves 4   5 mins   15 mins

Fishcakes

Potatoes can be cooked in many ways;
mashed, boiled, roasted, and baked. Bite into
these crunchy fishcakes and the creamy fish and
mash will melt in your mouth.

66

Ingredients

- 250g (9oz) undyed smoked haddock, trimmed
- 1 fresh bay leaf
- 300ml (10fl oz) milk
- 375g (¾lb) potatoes, unpeeled, boiled, and mashed
- 8 spring onions, finely chopped

- 100g (3½oz) tinned sweetcorn
- 4 eggs, hard-boiled, peeled and chopped
- 2 tbsp fresh parsley, chopped
- zest of 1 lemon
- 8 tbsp double cream
- 2 egg yolks
- 2 eggs

- 100g (3½oz) flour
- 125g (4½oz) breadcrumbs (see page 9 for instructions)
- 1 tbsp butter
- 2 tbsp olive oil
- salsa, to serve
- lemon wedges, to serve

Equipment

- shallow pan

- large mixing bowl
- fork
- spoon
- 2 small glass bowls
- whisk
- chopping board
- large shallow bowl
- large plate
- frying pan
- spatula

Cook the haddock fillets with the bay leaf and the milk in a shallow pan. Let them simmer for 5–10 minutes. Cool, then remove the fish's skin and any bones, and flake into chunks.

Mix the fish, potato, spring onions, sweetcorn, chopped eggs, parsley, and zest. In a small bowl, beat the cream with the egg yolks, and stir into the mixture.

Divide the mixture into four parts. Shape each part into a slightly flattened ball. Roll each fishcake in the flour on a plate. Shaking off any excess.

Crack two eggs into a small bowl and whisk. Transfer to a large shallow bowl. Dip each fishcake into the eggs so that they get egg all over the surface.

Dip egg-coated fishcake into the breadcrumbs and coat all over, then set aside. Repeat dipping into egg then breadcrumbs with the remaining fishcakes.

Heat the oil and butter in a frying pan and add the fishcakes carefully. Cook them gently for about 4–5 minutes on each side, or until golden brown.

Mashed potato pies

This dish is filling and nutritious. You can make it with beef, pork, lamb or soya mince. If you don't have four small dishes you can use one large dish instead.

1

Preheat the oven to 200°C (400°F/Gas 6). Peel and dice the onion and carrot. Crush the garlic.

2

Heat the oil and fry the beef for 4 minutes or until browned, stirring constantly. Add the onion, carrot, rosemary, and garlic and fry for 3–5 minutes.

3

Add the mushrooms, stock, tomato puree, Worcestershire sauce, and tomatoes. Bring to the boil and then reduce to a simmer for 20 minutes. Season.

4

Half-fill a pan with water and bring it to the boil. Peel and chop the potatoes and add them to the pan, with the salt. Boil for 12–15 minutes, or until soft.

5

Drain the potatoes in a colander and then tip them back into the saucepan. Mash the potatoes with the milk, butter, and half of the cheese.

6

Place the dishes on a baking tray and divide the meat filling equally between them. Top each with mashed potato and the remaining cheese. Bake for 25–30 minutes or until golden.

Ingredients

- 1 onion
- 1 carrot
- 1 garlic clove
- 1 tbsp olive oil
- 500g (1lb 2oz) lean minced beef
- 2 tsp rosemary, chopped, optional
- 125g (4½oz) mushrooms, quartered
- 150ml (5fl oz) beef stock
- 1 tbsp of tomato puree
- 2 tsp of Worcestershire sauce, optional
- 400g can chopped tomatoes

Topping

- 550g (1lb 3oz) potatoes
- 1 pinch of salt
- 2 tbsp milk
- 30g (1oz) unsalted butter
- 75g (2½oz) Cheddar cheese, grated

Equipment

- oven gloves
- chopping board
- peeler
- sharp knife
- garlic crusher
- 2 large saucepans
- wooden spoon
- colander
- masher
- four ovenproof dishes
- large baking tray
- fork
- dessert spoon

Serves 6   30 mins   40 mins

You can serve this dish with salsa, and tortilla chips.

Chilli con carne

This meal has a real kick to it so if you don't like your food too spicy then you should use less of the chilli. The meat and beans are full of protein and will fill you up. You can keep any leftovers in the fridge for the next day.

Ingredients

- 1½ large onions, diced
- 250g (9oz) lean minced beef
- 1 garlic clove, finely chopped
- ½ green chilli, finely chopped
- ¼ tsp chilli powder
- ¼ tsp paprika
- 400g can red kidney beans, drained and rinsed
- 1 bay leaf
- 400g can chopped tomatoes
- ½ tsp dried oregano
- basmati rice, to serve
- tortilla chips and salsa, to serve

Equipment

- frying pan
- wooden spoon
- colander
- glass bowl
- four small bowls or dishes for serving

1

Cook the onions and meat for 5 minutes. Stir in the garlic, chilli, chilli powder, and paprika, and cook for 5 minutes.

2

Add the kidney beans and bay leaf, fry for 2 minutes. Always be extra careful when near a hot stove. Ask an adult to help you.

3

Add the tomatoes and oregano. Bring to a boil, season with pepper, then simmer on a low heat for 40 minutes, stirring occasionally.

4

Ask an adult to cook the rice using the method on the packaging. Drain using a colander. Take the bay leaf out of the chilli before serving.

Ingredients

- 250g (9oz) beef mince
- 50g (1¾ oz) Parmesan cheese, freshly grated
- 30g (1oz) fresh breadcrumbs
- 1½ tbsp olive oil
- ½ garlic clove, crushed
- ½ onion finely chopped onion
- 1 egg
- 1 tsp dried oregano
- olive oil, for frying
- 16 mini bread rolls
- 2 tomatoes, thinly sliced
- lettuce leaves
- 400g jar of good quality tomato sauce or salsa

Equipment

- large glass bowl
- baking sheet
- greaseproof paper
- frying pan
- spatula
- chopping board
- knife
- skewers, to hold burgers together

Mini-burgers

These mini-burgers are hard to beat. Make them for your family and friends. They'll soon be asking you when you're going to make them again!

Prepare a baking sheet
with a piece of greaseproof paper. Use your hands to mix all the ingredients for the burgers (beef, cheese, breadcrumbs, oil, garlic, onion, egg, and oregano).

Form the mixture into balls
about the size of walnuts and then flatten them. Chill the meatballs in the fridge for 30 minutes. Wash your hands well after handling raw meat.

Fry the burgers in the oil on
a medium heat. Turn over after 5 minutes. Put a fork in the meat, if the juice is clear, then they're done.

Carefully cut the rolls in
half. Fill each roll with a cooked burger, a tomato slice, a lettuce leaf, and tomato sauce.

Variations

Add a slice of Cheddar cheese to each one to make cheese burgers!

Serves 6   30 mins   15 mins

BBQ chicken

On a summer's day you could cook this meal on an outdoor barbecue. The chicken also tastes good when cooked in a grill, as it's the marinade that gives it flavour.

Ingredients

- 2 tbsp tomato ketchup
- 2 tbsp soy sauce
- 2 tbsp fresh orange juice
- 1 tbsp sunflower oil
- 3 tbsp clear runny honey
- 1 garlic clove, crushed
- 1 tsp mustard
- 8 chicken drumsticks

Equipment

- small mixing bowl
- whisk
- kitchen paper
- sharp knife
- chopping board
- cling film
- oven gloves
- foil-lined grill tray
- tongs
- dessert spoon
- large dish, about 5cm (2in) deep

1

Place all the ingredients, except the chicken drumsticks, into a bowl and whisk them together. Pour the mixture into a large, shallow dish.

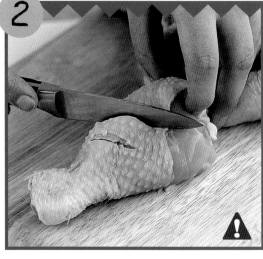

2

Pat the chicken pieces with kitchen towels. Make 3 deep cuts in each drumstick. This is known as scoring and helps the meat to soak up the marinade.

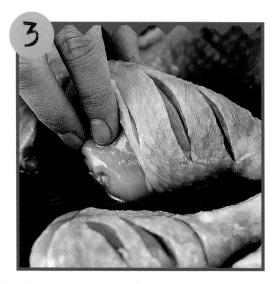

3

Place the chicken in the marinade and roll each piece until it is coated. Cover the dish with cling film and leave to marinate in the fridge for 1 hour.

4

Preheat the oven to 180°C (350°F/Gas 4). Lay the coated chicken (uncut side up) on a foil-lined grill pan. Put the marinade to one side. Bake the chicken for 20–25 minutes and baste it with leftover marinade halfway through.

Serves 4   75 mins   28-35 mins

5

Turn off the oven
and turn the grill on. Baste
the chicken pieces and finish
cooking them off under the
grill for 8–10 minutes.

6

Using tongs, turn the
chicken over halfway through
grilling and baste it with
marinade. This helps to keep
it moist.

Cook until
crispy on top

Four ways with Kebabs

Kebabs are fun and really easy to make.

Chicken satay

This is a popular kebab recipe. Always soak the wooden skewers in cold water for 30 minutes to prevent them from burning.

Ingredients

This recipe is for 4 people. It takes 20 minutes to prepare and 16 minutes to cook.

• 500g (1lb 2oz) chicken breasts

• $^1/_2$ lime, cut into wedges, to serve

• Follow the recipe on page 82 for the satay sauce

Method

• Make up the satay sauce in a large bowl and set aside. Save a small amount to use as a dip.

• Cut up the chicken breasts into large chunks 4cm (1$^1/_2$in) cubes and place into the large bowl of satay sauce. Marinate in the fridge for 1 hour.

• Thread the chicken chunks onto short skewers (or large skewers cut in half). Discard any remaining marinade.

• Place the kebabs on a grill pan and cook for about 8 minutes. Turn over and cook for another 8 minutes. Serve the chicken warm with the satay sauce for dipping and wedges of lime.

> To make sure the chicken is fully cooked, pierce it with a fork to see if the juices run clear.

Ingredients

This recipe is for 4 people. It takes 80 minutes to prepare and 20 minutes to cook.

For the kebabs

• 250g (9oz) firm tofu

• 2 small courgettes, each cut into 8 wedges

• 2 medium red onions, each cut into 8 wedges

• 1 medium red pepper, deseeded and cut into 16 chunks

For the marinade

• 2 tbsp olive oil

• 1 tbsp soy sauce

• 3 tbsp black bean sauce

• 1 tbsp clear runny honey

• 2 garlic cloves, crushed

• salad, to serve

Tofu chunks

This colourful kebab would make a perfect vegetarian option for a summer barbecue.

Method

• Cut the tofu into 16 cubes. Put the cubes into a dish with the courgettes, onions, and red pepper.

• Mix the ingredients for the marinade in a large dish. Season. Use a spoon to coat the tofu and vegetables in the marinade. Put in the fridge for 1 hour.

• Thread the vegetables and tofu onto 8 skewers.

• Place the kebabs on the grill and brush them with the marinade. Grill for 15–20 minutes, turning them halfway through and brushing them with more marinade.

yellow courgette

mushrooms

onions

halloumi cheese

aubergine

Try your own

Play around with combinations of ingredients to make up your own kebabs. Use the barbecue sauce from page 82 to create a beef and onion one. You can use the items pictured here, although not all on one kebab!

3

4

Lamb with mint yogurt

Lamb is delicious when flavoured with herbs and spices. You can make a mint and yogurt dip to accompany this classic kebab.

Ingredients

This recipe is for 4 people. It takes 20 minutes to prepare and 20 minutes to cook.

• 450g (1lb) minced lamb

• 1 small onion, finely chopped

• 1 garlic clove

• 1/2 tsp ground cinnamon

• 2 tsp ground cumin

• 1 tsp ground coriander

• olive oil, for brushing

• 1 tsp dried mint

• 1/2 lemon, to serve

• Follow the recipe on page 48 for the yogurt and mint dip

Method

• Put the lamb mince in a mixing bowl. Add the chopped onion, garlic, cinnamon, cumin, and coriander to the bowl. Stir the ingredients until they are all combined.

• Divide the lamb mixture into 12 pieces. Shape each one into a sausage and then thread them onto the skewers. Press or roll to lengthen the kebabs.

• Place the lamb kebabs onto the baking tray and brush them with oil. Grill them for about 5 minutes on each side, until golden. Transfer to a serving dish and sprinkle with mint.

Ingredients

This recipe is for 4 people. It takes 25 minutes to prepare and 15 minutes to cook.

For the marinade

• juice of 1 lemon

• juice of 1 lime

• 2 tbsp soy sauce

• 1 garlic clove, crushed

• 1 tsp light brown sugar

For the kebabs

• 1/2 red pepper

• 1/2 yellow pepper

• 8 cherry tomatoes

• 4 baby sweetcorn

• 150g (5 1/2 oz) cooked prawns

Prawn and peppers

This bright and colourful kebab is full of flavour. Squeeze lime juice on them to serve.

Method

• Make the marinade by mixing the ingredients together in a jug. Carefully cut the peppers and baby sweetcorn into chunks.

• Thread the vegetables and prawns onto the skewers. Place the kebabs into a rectangular dish. Pour the marinade over the kebabs. Put the kebabs into the fridge for an hour. Turn them over after 30 minutes.

• Grill the kebabs for 15 minutes. Baste the prawns every five minutes with the marinade (discard any leftover marinade).

Vegetable tart

This dish is best served cold.
It's perfect for a light evening meal
or lunch. Try it with some potato
salad and a green salad.

Serves 6   135 mins   65 mins

Equipment

- sieve
- mixing bowl
- knife
- fork
- tablespoon
- cling film
- rolling pin
- flan tin, loose-bottomed and fluted, approx. 20cm/8in diameter
- table knife
- greaseproof paper
- baking beans or dried kidney beans
- oven gloves
- jug
- whisk

Ingredients

- 225g (8oz) plain flour, plus extra for rolling
- a pinch of salt
- 90g (3oz) unsalted butter, diced
- 30g (1oz) vegetable fat or lard, cubed
- 2 tbsp water
- 100g (3½oz) red pepper, deseeded and diced
- 125g (4½oz) sweetcorn
- 125g (4½oz) peas
- 1 small leek, sliced and sautéed
- 2 eggs (beaten)
- 100ml (3½fl oz) milk
- 100ml (3½fl oz) cream
- 30g (1oz) Cheddar cheese, grated

Sift the flour and salt into a bowl. Stir in the butter and fat, until coated with flour. Rub the fats into the flour.

Once the mixture looks like crumbs, add the water, drop by drop, and stir with a knife. When the crumbs start to come together, gather the pastry in your hands.

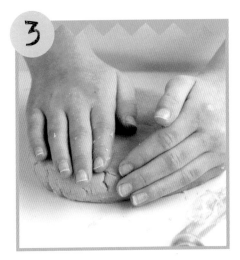

Shape the pastry into a smooth disc and wrap it in cling film. Chill it for 1 hour in the fridge, or until firm. Grease your tin and lightly flour your work top.

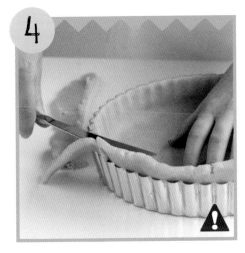

Roll out the pastry so that it is slightly bigger than the tin. Gently press it into the tin and use a knife to trim off the excess. Use a fork to prick the base and chill it again for 15 minutes. Preheat the oven to 200°C (400°F/Gas 6).

Cover the tart with 2 layers of greaseproof paper and add the baking beans. Bake for 15 minutes, remove the paper and beans and bake for a further 5 minutes. This technique is called baking blind and it helps the pastry stay firm when the wet filling is added.

Ask an adult to turn the oven down to 180°C (350°F/Gas 4). Scatter the ham and vegetables over the base. Whisk the eggs, milk, and cream together and pour into the tart. Sprinkle over the cheese and bake for 45 minutes. Allow the tart to set and cool before serving.

Tomato and aubergine layers

Slow roasted tomatoes are chewy, juicy, and tasty. Everyone who tries this dish will love the combination of textures and flavours.

Ingredients

- 6 large ripe tomatoes, cut in half
- 2 garlic cloves, finely chopped
- 1 tbsp dried oregano
- 8 tbsp extra-virgin olive oil
- 1 large aubergine, thinly sliced
- pinch of smoked paprika
- 8 tbsp natural yogurt
- 2 tbsp runny honey
- 4 tbsp sliced almonds, toasted

Equipment

- baking tray
- spoon
- colander
- large bowl
- griddle pan
- 4 serving dishes

1

Lay the tomatoes cut-side up on the tray. In a small bowl, mix the garlic and oregano, half of the olive oil, and season with salt and pepper. Spoon it over the tomatoes.

2

Preheat the oven to (150°C 300°F/Gas 2). Bake the tomatoes for 2–3 hours. When ready, they should be slightly shrunk, but still a brilliant red colour. Allow to cool.

3

Layer the slices of aubergine in a colander, sprinkling a little salt between each layer. Leave for 30 minutes then rinse well with water and dry.

4

Place the aubergine slices in a large bowl, pour over the rest of the olive oil, and sprinkle with a little paprika. Toss together with your hands.

Serves 4   40 mins   190 mins

5

Heat a ridged griddle pan, then add a single layer of the aubergine slices. Cook each side until tender. Place the slices on a plate. Repeat for the other slices.

6

To serve, layer the tomatoes and aubergines in 4 dishes. Drizzle two tablespoons of yogurt and half a tbsp of honey over each dish. Sprinkle half a tablespoon of almonds over each portion.

Four ways with sauces

Try these simple and versatile sauces.

1

Chunky tomato sauce

This sauce is hearty and full of flavour. It can be used in a lasagne if you double the quantities or as a simple sauce for a pasta dish.

Ingredients

This recipe is for 4 people. It takes 3 minutes to prepare and 5 minutes to cook.

• 1 onion

• 1 garlic clove

• 2 tbsp olive oil

• 400g tinned tomatoes

• 1 tbsp tomato puree

Method

• Chop the onion into small pieces and crush the garlic clove.

• Pour the oil into a saucepan and add the onion and garlic. Fry gently for 2 minutes or until the onion is golden.

• Add the tinned tomatoes and puree to the saucepan, stir and cook for 3 minutes.

2

Crunchy satay sauce

You can use smooth peanut butter for this classic sauce, but crunchy peanut butter gives it a better texture.

Ingredients

This recipe is for 4 people. It takes 5 minutes to prepare and 6 minutes to cook.

• 1½ onions

• 3cm (1½ in) cube fresh ginger

• 3 garlic clove

• 4½ tbsp vegetable oil

• 3 tbsp soy sauce

• 9 tbsp water

• 4½ tbsp light brown sugar

• 15 tbsp crunchy peanut butter

• juice of 2 limes

Method

• Peel the onion and chop it very finely.

• Peel the ginger and grate it coarsely, then peel and crush the garlic.

• Heat the oil in a saucepan. Cook the onion gently for 3 minutes or until soft. Add the ginger and garlic and cook for a few minutes. Let the mixture cool down.

• Put the onion mixture, soy sauce, water, sugar, peanut butter, and lime juice in a bowl and whisk.

• This recipe is perfect for chicken kebabs (see page 76).

Get these tools...

As the name suggests, a saucepan is for making sauces in. You will need these items in order to make most sauces. The wooden spoon is for stirring and the whisk is for blending the ingredients together.

saucepan

wooden spoon

whisk

knife

3

4

Cheesy white sauce

This sauce is often used in lasagne (see 58–59). You can also put it on pasta and add cooked bacon to make a cheesy, creamy pasta.

Ingredients

This recipe is for 6 people (when used in a lasagne). It takes 5 minutes to prepare and 6 minutes to cook.

· 60g (2oz) unsalted butter

· 30g (1oz) plain flour

· 500ml (16fl oz) warm milk

· 60g (2oz) Parmesan cheese, grated

Method

● Over a low heat, melt the butter in a small pan.

● Stir in the flour and cook for 1 minute. Gradually whisk in the milk. Stir and continue heating until thickened.

● Add in the cheese and season. Stir until the cheese is well mixed into the sauce.

Barbecue sauce

Tasty and sweet, this sauce uses the natural sugars from oranges and honey to give it a delicious flavour.

Ingredients

This recipe is for 6 people. It takes 10 minutes to prepare and works perfectly for a marinade.

· 2 garlic cloves

· 4 tbsp tomato ketchup

· 4 tbsp soy sauce

· 4 tbsp fresh orange juice

· 2 tbsp sunflower oil

· 6 tbsp clear, runny honey

· 2 tsp mustard

Method

● Crush the garlic cloves and put in a glass bowl.

● Add the ketchup, soy sauce, and orange juice to the bowl and mix well with a wooden spoon.

● Pour in the sunflower oil, runny honey, and mustard. Mix all the ingredients for 2 minutes or until everything has blended into a sauce.

● This recipe has double quantities of the BBQ chicken recipe on pages 74–75. Use it as a marinade to flavour meat or vegetables.

Mixed bean stir-fry

This vegetarian stir-fry is incredibly tasty and quick to cook. The dessicated coconut and cashew nuts give it a crunchy texture and delicious flavour.

Serves 4   30 mins   10 mins

Ingredients

- 50g (1¾oz) dessicated coconut, unsweetened
- 2 tbsp sunflower oil
- 1 garlic clove, sliced
- 6 spring onions, chopped
- 1 fennel bulb, sliced, core removed
- 500g (1lb 2oz) French and runner beans, thinly sliced
- 2 tbsp soy sauce
- 1 tbsp rice vinegar
- 100g (3½oz) beansprouts
- 1 tbsp fresh coriander, chopped
- 200g (7oz) wholewheat noodles
- 1 tbsp sesame seeds
- 75g (2½oz) unsalted cashew nuts

1

Place the coconut in a bowl of warm water, cover, and leave for 20 minutes. Strain the coconut through a sieve, pressing it against the sides.

2

Heat the oil in a large frying pan or wok. Add the garlic, onion, and fennel. Using a wooden spoon stir all the time for about 2 minutes.

3

Add your sliced beans and fry quickly, stirring all the time. Pour on the soy sauce and vinegar. Stir in, then remove the pan from the heat.

4

Add the beansprouts to the stir-fry. Sprinkle on the coconut and coriander. Then give the mixture another good stir. Mmm! Smells good.

5

Cook some noodles following the instructions on the packet. Drain the noodles using a colander, then spoon them into your serving bowls.

6

Spoon out the stir-fry on top of the noodles. After roasting the cashew nuts and sesame seeds, sprinkle over and serve.

Ingredients

- 300g (10½oz) lean beef, cut into thin strips
- 1 tbsp sunflower oil
- 1 red pepper, deseeded and cut into thin strips
- 6 baby corn, halved
- 75g (2½oz) mangetout
- 3 spring onions, sliced on the diagonal
- 2 cloves garlic, chopped
- 2 tsp grated fresh ginger
- 4 tbsp fresh orange juice

Marinade

- 6 tbsp hoisin sauce
- 2 tbsp soy sauce
- 1 tbsp runny clear honey
- 1 tsp sesame oil

Equipment

- small sharp knife
- chopping board
- spoon
- shallow dish
- wok or large frying pan
- spatula or wooden spoon
- tongs

Rainbow beef

Stir-frying is a quick and easy way to make a colourful and nutritious meal. You can serve it on its own or eat it with rice or noodles.

Put the marinade ingredients in a shallow dish. Mix them together and then add the beef strips. Coat them in the marinade, cover, and set aside for 1 hour.

Heat the sunflower oil in a wok or frying pan. Remove the beef from the marinade using tongs and carefully put it into the wok or frying pan.

Stirring continuously, fry the beef on a high heat for 1½ minutes or until browned all over. Remove the beef using the tongs and set aside.

Add a little more oil to the wok if it looks dry. Add the red pepper, baby corn, mangetout, and spring onions. Stir-fry for 2 minutes.

Serves 4   80 mins   10 mins

Add the garlic, ginger, beef, and leftover marinade and stir-fry for 1 minute. Pour in the orange juice, and cook stirring, for another minute.

Variations

Strips of pork and chicken are a good alternative to the beef, or you could try prawns or tofu. For the best flavour, it's important to marinate them first.

Marinated chicken

The chicken in this recipe is marinated so that it absorbs the curry flavour. If you want a stronger flavour you can marinate the meat for longer than 30 minutes.

In a bowl, mix the tomato puree, oil, and curry powder together to make a paste. Add the lemon juice and half the yogurt to make the marinade.

Carefully cut each chicken breast into cubes of about 2.5cm (1"). Always wash your hands after handling raw meat.

Stir the chicken into the marinade, season with salt and pepper, and cover the bowl. Leave the chicken to marinate in the fridge for 30 minutes.

Place the frying pan over a medium to high heat and fry the chicken for 3–4 minutes. The chicken will change colour but it will not be cooked.

Add the sultanas and almonds and cook for 3–4 minutes. Before serving, cut a piece of chicken in half. If there is no trace of pink, it is cooked.

To shred the lettuce, roll up the leaves and carefully cut them into thin slices. Serve the chicken with the shredded lettuce, naan bread, and mango chutney.

Ingredients

- 1 tsp tomato puree
- 2 tbsp vegetable oil
- 1 tbsp curry powder
- juice of ½ lemon
- 125g (4½oz) natural yogurt

- 2 chicken breasts, skinless and boneless
- 30g (1oz) sultanas, optional
- 30g (1oz) flaked almonds, optional

To serve

- 1-2 Little Gem lettuces
- naan bread
- 2 tbsp mango chutney, optional

Equipment

- mixing bowl
- dessert spoon
- 2 chopping boards
- 2 sharp knives
- frying pan
- wooden spatula

Serves 4   50 mins   10 mins

Four ways with roast vegetables

Each of these dishes can accompany a main meal.

1

Reds and greens

This vegetable medley is colourful and has a slight crunch. It could be paired with the Rice balls or Griddled chicken.

Ingredients

This recipe is for 4 people when served as a side dish. It takes 8 minutes to prepare and 50–60 minutes to cook.

- 2 red onions
- 2 whole raw beetroots, peeled
- ½ head of broccoli
- 12 cherry tomatoes
- 1 tbsp olive oil

Method

- Preheat the oven to 200°C (400°F/Gas 6).

- On a chopping board use a sharp knife to carefully cut the red onion into large chunks, slice the beetroot into large wedges, and cut the florets off the half head of broccoli.

- Place the beetroot into a roasting tin or oven-proof dish and use your hands to toss the vegetables with oil. Cook for 20 minutes.

- Add the remaining ingredients and cook for a further 30–40 minutes.

2

Sweet potato and parsnip

Perfect on a cold day, this option could be eaten with the lamb or sausage hotpot.

Ingredients

This recipe is for 4 people when served as a side dish. It takes 5 minutes to prepare and 50 minutes to cook.

- 4 large sweet potatoes, peeled
- 4 parsnips, peeled
- 1 tbsp olive oil

Method

- Preheat the oven to 200°C (400°F/Gas 6).

- On a chopping board use a sharp knife to carefully cut the parsnips into large chunks and slice the sweet potatoes into large wedges.

- Put the parsnips and potatoes into a roasting tin or an oven-proof dish and use your hands to toss the vegetables with oil.

- Roast in the over for 50 minutes or until the vegetables are golden.

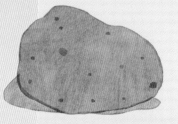

Try your own

There are plenty of other vegetables that taste delicious when roasted and work well as a side for any main dish. Try out these other ingredients.

mushrooms

butternut squash

tomatoes

leeks

olives

3

Pepper medley

Roasted garlic is really tasty and roasted peppers are juicy and full of flavour. This dish would sit well with the Marinated chicken meal.

Ingredients

This recipe is for 4 people when served as a side dish. It takes 8 minutes to prepare and 40 minutes to cook.

• 1 green pepper

• 1 yellow pepper

• 1 red pepper

• 1 orange pepper

• 1 garlic clove

• 2 small courgettes

• 1 tbsp olive oil

Method

• Preheat the oven to 200°C (400°F/Gas 6).

• On a chopping board use a sharp knife to slice the peppers into thin strips and the garlic in half.

• Carefully cut the courgette into thick slices.

• Place all the ingredients into a roasting tin or oven-proof and use your hands to toss the vegetables with oil.

• Cook for 40 minutes.

4

Roast potato and carrot

This is a classic choice of roasted vegetables that often gets served with chicken. It can help add carbohydrates to a lighter meal.

Ingredients

This recipe is for 4 people when served as a side dish. It takes 5 minutes to prepare and 50 minutes to cook.

• 12 Chantenay carrots, or 5 regular carrots

• 2 large potatoes, peeled

Method

• Preheat the oven to 200°C (400°F/Gas 6).

• On a chopping board use a sharp knife to quarter the potatoes and cut the carrots into thick wedges.

• Scatter the potatoes and carrots into a roasting tin or oven-proof dish and use your hands to toss the vegetables with oil.

• Cook for 50 minutes or until the vegetables are golden.

Ingredients

- 1.5kg (3lb 3oz) whole chicken
- 75g (2½oz) unsalted butter, softened
- ½ a lemon and 1 tsp lemon zest
- 1 tbsp fresh thyme leaves, plus 2 sprigs
- 1 large onion, chopped
- 8 mini carrots
- 1 garlic bulb
- 250ml (8fl oz) vegetable stock

To Serve

- 12 broccoli florets, boiled and drained
- 4 potatoes, chopped into quarters and roasted (see also page 91)
- 16 mini carrots, roasted (see also page 91)
- 250ml (8fl oz) gravy

Equipment

- chopping board
- kitchen paper
- small mixing bowl
- 2 dessert spoons
- sharp knife
- string
- roasting tin
- oven gloves
- large wooden chopping board
- carving knife

Everyone loves a traditional roast lunch or dinner. Once you've mastered this classic recipe, you'll be able to use it for the rest of your life. You'll definitely impress your family when you make it.

Preheat the oven to 200°C (400°F/ Gas 6). Rinse the chicken, inside and out, under cold running water. Place it on a board and then pat dry, inside and out, with kitchen paper.

To make the stuffing, mix the softened butter with the thyme leaves, and lemon zest in a bowl and season with salt and pepper. Spoon it inside the chicken, along with the lemon and thyme sprigs.

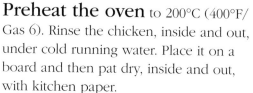

Put the chicken into a roasting tin on a bed of onions, carrot, garlic and vegetable stock. Roast it for 1 hour and 20 minutes, or until golden brown. Baste the meat after 30 minutes and then every 15 minutes after that.

Carefully transfer the cooked chicken to a rack (you might want to ask an adult for help) and leave to rest for 10–15 minutes before carving. Serve with broccoli, roasted potatoes and carrots, and a generous helping of gravy.

Serves 4   30 mins   80 mins

Extras

Use the recipe on page 91 for
roasting potatoes and carrots.
Boil the broccoli florets for
5 minutes, drain and serve.
Make up 250ml (8fl oz) of
gravy to serve with
your meal.

Griddled chicken

Food has an wonderful texture and finish to it when it's been cooked in a griddle pan. Always make sure you cook the meat thoroughly. You can eat this dish hot or cold.

Serves 4   45 mins   25 mins

Ingredients

- 2 tsp paprika
- 5 tbsp olive oil
- 4 skinless chicken breasts, each about 150g (5½oz)
- 400g (14oz) baby new potatoes, cut in half if necessary
- 2 spring onions, finely chopped

- 8 cherry tomatoes, halved
- 3 tbsp chopped fresh mint
- 1 tbsp lemon juice

Equipment

- large shallow dish
- tablespoon
- cling film

- griddle pan
- tongs
- small sharp knife
- chopping board
- medium saucepan
- colander
- large glass bowl

1

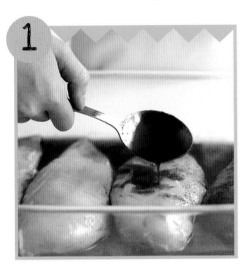

Mix the paprika and 3 tablespoons of olive oil in a large dish. Add the chicken and spoon over the marinade. Cover with cling film and chill for 30 minutes.

2

Heat a griddle pan until it is very hot. Reduce the heat to medium and place 2 chicken breasts in the pan. Griddle for 6 minutes on one side.

3

Carefully turn the chicken over using tongs. Spoon over a little of the marinade and then cook for 6 minutes, or until cooked through. Griddle the remaining chicken.

4

Put the potatoes in a medium saucepan and cover with water. Bring to the boil and cook the potatoes for 10 minutes or until they are tender.

5

Drain the potatoes and leave them to cool in a bowl. Put them in the bowl. Add the mint.

6

Mix the olive oil and lemon juice together, using a fork. Then pour the dressing over the salad and stir well to mix it in.

SWEET THINGS

Ingredients

- 225g (8oz) ready-made shortcrust pastry
- 150g (5½ oz) mascarpone cheese
- ½ tsp vanilla extract
- 2 tbsp icing sugar
- 175g (6oz) strawberries or other soft fruit
- 4 tbsp redcurrant jelly
- 15ml (1 tbsp) water

Equipment

- rolling pin
- 9cm (3½") fluted cutter
- 12-hole bun tin
- baking parchment
- dried beans or chickpeas
- oven gloves
- cooling rack
- small mixing bowl
- wooden spoon
- sieve
- chopping board
- sharp knife
- teaspoon
- small saucepan
- pastry brush

Strawberry tarts

These pretty pastries taste as good as they look! You can also make them with other types of soft fruit.

Makes 8   20 mins   14 mins

Preheat the oven to 200°C (400°F/Gas 6). Thinly roll out the pastry, then using the fluted cutter, cut out 8 circles. Press the pastry circles into a bun tin.

Line the cases with baking parchment and fill them with dried beans. Cook for 10 minutes, then remove the beans. Return to the oven for 3 minutes. Cool in the tin.

Transfer the cases to a cooling rack. Place the cheese and vanilla extract in a mixing bowl. Sift over the icing sugar, then beat with a wooden spoon until smooth.

Place the strawberries on a chopping board. Remove the green stalks from the strawberries. Then use a knife to cut them in half or quarters if they are large.

When the pastry cases are completely cool, use a teaspoon to fill them with the mascarpone and vanilla mixture. Arrange the strawberries over the top.

Place the redcurrant jelly in a small pan with the water and cook over a low heat, stirring until the jelly has dissolved. Brush this over the strawberries.

Four ways with cookies

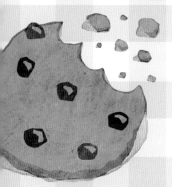

Everyone enjoys making cookies and everyone loves to eat them. Try out these tasty combinations or come up with your own.

Basic cookie dough

This recipe is for 8 people (which allows for 2 cookies each). It takes 40 minutes to prepare and 15 minutes to cook.

- 100g (3½oz) butter, at room temperature
- 1 egg
- 125g (4½oz) caster sugar
- ½ tsp vanilla extract
- 150g (5½oz) self-raising flour

Equipment

- 2 baking trays
- baking parchment
- large glass bowl
- electric whisk
- wooden spoon

1 Hazelnut delights

Hazelnuts have a brilliant flavour and crunch. Alternatively, you could try the same quantity of another nut. Do you like peanuts, walnuts, pecans, or pistachios?

Ingredients

(to add to basic dough recipe above)
- 75g (2½ oz) hazelnuts, cut in half

Top tips

- Toast the nuts under the grill for 2 minutes before you stir them into the dough mixture.
- Wrap up a pile of cookies in baking parchment and tie it with ribbon to make a parcel to give to someone.

2 Cranberry chews

You can play around with trying the same quantity of another dried fruit. Which is your favourite? Try raisins, mangoes, apples, blueberries or cherries.

Ingredients

(to add to basic dough recipe above)
- 45g (1½oz) white chocolate, broken into small pieces
- 45g (1½oz) dried cranberries, finely chopped

Top tips

- Mix the ingredients really well so that the cranberries and white chocolate don't all sit together. They need to be spread out well in each cookie.
- Serve the cookies with a glass of milk for each person.

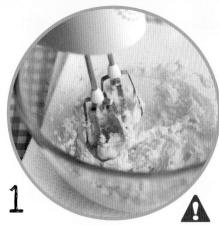

1

Preheat the oven to 180°C (350°F/Gas 4). Line two trays with baking parchment. In a large bowl, use an electric whisk to whisk the butter and egg together. Mix in the sugar and vanilla.

2

Work in the flour with a spoon until the mixture forms a soft dough, then mix in your additional ingredients from one of the recipes below. Chill in the fridge for 30 minutes.

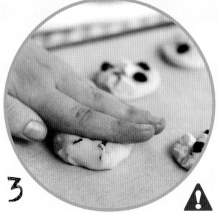

3

Roll the dough into about 16 balls and place on the baking trays, leaving space around each ball. Flatten the balls slightly and bake in the oven for 15 minutes or until golden. Cool them on a wire rack.

3

Traditional chocolate

This is a classic cookie that everyone likes. Why not try chunks of milk chocolate or chunks of white chocolate instead? You could add a twist to this cookie by adding nuts.

Ingredients

(to add to dough recipe above)
· 75g (2½oz) dark chocolate, broken into small pieces

Top tips

• Make the chunks quite big so that they are nice and gooey when you bite into a cookie.

• On a cold day you could make hot chocolate to serve with the cookies for a real chocolatey treat.

4

Apricots and cinnamon

There are other spices you can try instead of cinnamon. Put in a quarter of a teaspoon of mixed spice or an eighth of a teaspoon of ground ginger. You can substitute apricots for raisins or sultanas.

Ingredients

(to add to basic dough recipe above)
· 75g (2½oz) dried apricots, finely chopped
· ¼ tsp ground cinnamon

Top tips

• Make the apricot pieces small so that they are scattered well throughout each cookie.

• Store in a tin for a couple of days, if they don't get eaten before then!

Cupcakes

Whether you go for delicately or boldly decorated cupcakes, make sure you have enough toppings to choose from. Tie in with a theme if they're for a party.

Ingredients

- 150g (5½oz) unsalted butter, softened
- 150g (5½oz) caster sugar
- 150g (5½oz) self-raising flour
- 3 eggs, whisked
- ½ tsp vanilla extract

Icing and decoration

- 225g (8oz) icing sugar, sifted
- 2-3 tbsp hot water
- 3 different food colourings
- edible crystallized flowers, sugar strands hundreds and thousands, or sweets

Equipment

- 2 x 12-hole bun tins
- 20 paper cases
- 5 mixing bowls
- wooden spoon
- 2 metal spoons
- cooling rack
- sieve
- knife

Line 2 bun tins with 20 paper cases – there are plenty of different designs to choose from. Ask an adult to preheat the oven to 180°C (350°F/Gas 4).

Place the butter, sugar, self-raising flour, eggs, and vanilla extract in a bowl and beat with a wooden spoon until pale in colour and creamy.

Divide between the paper cases. Bake for 15 minutes until golden and just firm. Cool in the tin for 5 minutes, then transfer to a cooling rack to cool.

Trim any pointed tops to make a flat surface – then the icing will sit better, ready for your decorations.

Makes 20   30 mins   15 mins

DISPLAY ON A STAND

Mix the icing sugar in a large bowl, gradually beat in enough water to give a smooth thick icing, which coats the back of a spoon.

Transfer the icing mixture to 3 individual bowls and add a few drops of food colouring to each. Spoon onto the cakes and top with decorations. Allow to set.

Sponge

The simplest but still the most delicious cake, sponge can be done Victoria style, as here, or zested up with some zingy lemon in the sponge and filling.

Serves 8   10 mins   30 mins

Grease the cake tins so that the sponge cakes don't stick. Ask an adult to preheat the oven to 180°C (350°F, Gas 4).

Place the butter, sugar, eggs and vanilla extract in a large bowl and sift over the flour and baking powder. Using an electric or hand whisk, beat all the ingredients together until thick.

Divide the mixture between the 2 tins, levelling the tops with the back of a tablespoon. Bake in the centre of the oven for 25–30 minutes, or until risen and firm to the touch.

Leave the cakes to cool in the tins for 5–10 minutes, then turn them out onto a cooling rack and allow them to cool completely.

To make the filling, place the butter, icing sugar, vanilla extract, and milk in a mixing bowl. Beat them together with a wooden spoon until smooth and creamy.

Use a spatula to spread jam on the flat side of one of the cakes and put on a cake stand. Spread the flat side of the other with the buttercream and pop on top. Finish off with a dusting of icing sugar.

Ingredients

- 175g (6oz) butter, softened
- 175g (6oz) caster sugar
- 3 eggs, beaten
- 1 tsp vanilla extract
- 175g (6oz) self-raising flour
- 1 tsp baking powder
- 4 tbsp raspberry or strawberry jam
- icing sugar, for dusting

For the buttercream

- 50g (2oz) butter, softened
- 125g (4½oz) icing sugar
- ½ tsp vanilla extract
- 2 tsp milk

Equipment

- 2 x 20cm (8in) round cake tins
- baking parchment
- large mixing bowl
- sieve
- electric or hand whisk
- tablespoon
- oven gloves
- cooling rack
- mixing bowl
- wooden spoon
- spatula

Makes 15   15 mins   10 mins

Ingredients

- 350g (12oz) plain flour
- 2 tsp ground ginger
- 1 tsp bicarbonate of soda
- 125g (4½oz) butter, diced
- 150g (5½oz) soft dark brown sugar
- 4 tbsp golden syrup
- 1 egg, beaten
- sweets, currants, and icing, for decoration

Equipment

- 2 large baking trays
- baking parchment
- large mixing bowl
- wooden spoon
- rolling pin
- cutters of your choice
- oven gloves

Gingerbread

Fill your house with the wondrous smell

of baking gingerbread. Search out some unusual cutters to make your shapes stand out from the crowd.

1

Ask an adult to preheat the oven to 180°C (350°F/Gas 4). Line 2 large baking trays with baking parchment. If you only have 1 tray, you will need to cook the biscuits in a couple of batches.

2

Place the flour, ginger, and bicarbonate of soda in a large bowl. Stir the ingredients together with a wooden spoon until they are thoroughly mixed.

3

Rub the butter into the mixture using your fingertips. Continue rubbing in the butter until the mixture resembles fine breadcrumbs. Stir in the sugar.

4

Stir in the golden syrup and egg until the mixture starts to come together in a dough. Next, tip the dough mixture out onto a lightly floured surface and knead it until smooth.

5

Roll out the dough on a lightly floured surface to a thickness of 5mm (¼in), then using your cutters, cut out the shapes. Re-roll the leftover dough and cut out more biscuits until it's all used.

6

Place the biscuits on the baking trays and bake in the preheated oven for 9–10 minutes or until golden. Allow the biscuits to cool on the trays. Decorate with sweets, currants, and icing.

Brownies

A real crowd-pleasing treat, brownies taste divine whether made with white, milk, or plain chocolate. If you're feeling hungry, just cut them into larger pieces and share out.

Makes 16   25 mins   25 mins

Ingredients

- 90g (3oz) plain chocolate
- 150g (5½oz) unsalted butter, diced, plus extra for greasing
- 125g (4½oz) plain flour
- 15g (½oz) cocoa powder
- ½ tsp baking powder
- a pinch of salt
- 2 eggs
- 300g (10oz) soft light brown sugar
- 1 tsp vanilla extract
- 100g (3½oz) pecan nuts, chopped, optional

Equipment

- baking tin (20 x 15cm or 8 x 6in)
- scissors
- pencil
- baking parchment
- 3 medium bowls
- wooden spoon
- small saucepan
- sieve
- spatula
- palette knife
- oven gloves

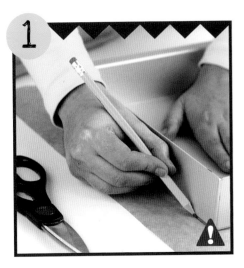

1

Grease and line the base of the baking tin with baking parchment (see instructions on page 11). Ask and adult to preheat the oven to 180°C (350°F/Gas 4).

2

Break the chocolate into a bowl and add the chunks of butter. Melt the butter and chocolate over a saucepan of barely simmering water, stirring occasionally.

3

Remove the bowl from the heat and allow the chocolate to cool slightly. In a separate bowl sieve the flour, cocoa powder, baking powder, and salt.

4

In a third bowl, beat the eggs and then add the sugar and vanilla extract. Stir the ingredients together until they are just combined.

5

Fold the melted chocolate into the beaten egg mixture using a spatula. Then gently fold in the flour mixture and nuts, if using. You shouldn't be able to see any flour once it's all mixed together.

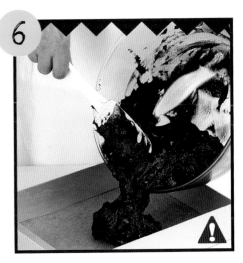

6

Spoon the mixture into the tin, smooth the top with a palette knife, and bake for 25 minutes. Allow it to cool in the tin before cutting into squares.

Ingredients

- 140g (5oz) plain flour
- 2 tsp baking powder
- ½ tsp bicarbonate of soda
- 85g (3oz) light brown sugar
- 50g (1¾oz) roasted hazelnuts, chopped
- 100g (3½oz) carrot, grated
- 100g (3½oz) unsulphured apricots, chopped finely
- 1 tbsp poppy seeds
- ½ tsp ground cinnamon
- 100g (3½oz) porridge oats
- zest of 2 oranges
- 200ml (7fl oz) buttermilk or milk and 1 tbsp lemon juice
- 1 egg, beaten
- 3 tbsp melted butter
- a pinch of salt
- juice of 1 large orange

For the topping

- 2 tbsp soft brown sugar
- 50g (1½oz) porridge oats
- 1 tbsp melted butter

Equipment

- small glass bowl
- baking sheet
- chopping board
- sharp knife
- large glass bowl
- spoon
- muffin cases
- muffin tray

Carrot and orange muffins

The versatile carrot can be savoury or sweet, as in these delicious muffins – a perfect snack or lunchbox treat.

Ask an adult to preheat the oven to 200°C (400°F/Gas 6). To make the topping, mix together the ingredients in a bowl. Sprinkle the mixture onto a baking sheet. Bake for 5 minutes, then leave to cool.

In a large bowl, mix the flour, baking powder, bicarbonate of soda, and sugar. Then, add the nuts, carrot, apricots, poppy seeds, cinnamon, oats, and orange zest. Mix together well.

In another bowl, use a spoon to mix the buttermilk, egg, butter, salt, and orange juice. Pour this liquid mixture onto the bowl of dry ingredients.

Stir the two mixtures together using a spoon. Be careful not to over mix as this will "knock out" all the air. In fact, the lumpier the mixture, the better the muffins will be!

Makes 8 20 mins 25 mins

Flavour try-outs

For extra zing use lemons instead of oranges. Or make a hole with your finger (after step 5) and pop in a chunk of white chocolate for a lovely gooey centre.

5

Place 8 paper cases into a muffin tray. Spoon the mixture into the cases, filling them two-thirds full.

6

Sprinkle the crumbly topping over the muffins. Bake in the preheated oven for about 25–30 minutes until well risen and golden. Leave to cool.

Extra recipe idea

Try out this recipe with 300g (10oz) of your favourite ingredients, such as bananas, strawberries, meringues, raspberries, or a chopped-up bar of chocolate.

110

Frozen yogurt

Create your new favourite icy alternative to ice cream by experimenting with flavours. You'll make enough for plenty of friends to cool down on a hot summer's day!

8-12 scoops   4 hrs 20 mins

1

Carefully chop the fudge and honeycomb into tiny pieces on a board, and then break up the cookies into slightly larger pieces.

2

Pour the cream into a mixing bowl and sift in the icing sugar. Lightly whip the cream to soft peaks. (You could use an electric or a hand whisk.)

3

Gently fold the yogurt, honeycomb, fudge, cookies, and marshmallow pieces into the cream mixture using a plastic spatula or a metal spoon.

4

Spoon the mixture into the tubs, cover, and freeze. After 2 hours in the freezer, stir the mixture to prevent ice crystals forming and then freeze for at least 2 hours more. It'll then be ready to serve. If it thaws, do not refreeze.

Ingredients

- 85g (3oz) soft fudge
- 60g (2oz) honeycomb, optional
- 85g (3oz) chocolate chunk cookies
- 150ml (5fl oz) double cream
- 30g (1oz) icing sugar
- 500g (1lb 2oz) natural yogurt
- 60g (2oz) mini marshmallows

Equipment

- chopping board
- sharp knife
- mixing bowl
- sieve
- whisk
- spatula or metal spoon
- 2 plastic tubs with lids

Mint chocolate pots

These luxury, rather grown-up, desserts are super-chocolatey but with a minty kick. Dress them up with a stencilled shape of icing sugar or cocoa.

Ingredients

- 300ml (10fl oz) double cream
- small bunch of mint, chopped
- 120ml (4fl oz) milk
- 175g (6oz) milk chocolate, broken into small pieces
- 3 egg yolks
- 1 tbsp icing sugar, plus extra for dusting
- cocoa powder, for dusting, optional

Equipment

- chopping board
- sharp knife
- 2 saucepans
- mixing bowl
- wooden spoon
- whisk
- sieve
- roasting tin
- 4 ramekins
- card, pencil, scissors

Ask an adult to preheat the oven to 150°C (300°F/Gas 2). Pour the cream into a small pan, and add the mint. Heat gently until nearly boiling, then remove from heat, cover, and leave for 30 minutes.

Meanwhile, pour the milk into another small pan and heat gently. Remove from the heat and stir in the chocolate pieces until melted and the mixture is smooth.

Whisk the egg yolks and sugar together and add the chocolatey milk and the minty cream. Mix well, then strain the mixture through a fine sieve to remove the mint.

Pour the mixture into 4 ramekins stood in a roasting tin. Add hot water until it's halfway up the outside of the cups. Bake for 45–60 minutes. Let them cool and then refrigerate for a few hours. Decorate just before serving, if you want.

Stencils

Make a stencil out of card – stars, circles, and flowers work well – and sift some icing sugar, or cocoa powder, on top for a knock-out decoration.

Serves 4   45 mins   45-60 mins

Fridge cake

A no-cook cake, what could be easier? And you get to do some bashing. This cake uses nuts, but you could swap it for other types of dried fruit, such as cranberries, if you prefer.

Ingredients

- 450g (1lb) digestive biscuits
- 150g (5½oz) butter
- 500g (1lb 2oz) dark chocolate, broken into pieces
- 2 tbsp golden syrup
- 50g (1¾oz) raisins
- 50g (1¾oz) almonds, chopped

Equipment

- rolling pin
- plastic bag
- mixing bowl
- saucepan
- wooden spoon
- 18 x 18cm (7 x 7in) tin
- baking parchment
- potato masher
- sharp knife
- chopping board

Place the biscuits in a plastic bag and bash them with a rolling pin. Don't break them too finely, though. You need chunks still, not dust.

Melt the butter, chocolate, and syrup in a bowl over a saucepan of hot water. Stir together to make a shiny mixture. Remove from the heat.

When the bowl is cool to touch, stir in the biscuits, raisins, and almonds. Make sure all the ingredients are mixed really well. Now, line the tin with baking parchment.

Use a masher to press the mixture into the tin and put in the refrigerator to harden. Cut into 24 pieces. If you like, freeze some in an airtight container and eat within a few months.

Makes 24   10 mins   1 hour

with a twist

For a crackly surprise, add 50g (1³/₄oz) of popping candy after step 3. Don't measure it out until the moment you need it or all the "popping-ness" will go.

Meringue crowns

These beautiful desserts are impressive and the good news is they are easier to make than they look! Each crown is large, and serves 2 people, so invite your friends round to share in the sweetness.

Serves 6 | 45 mins | 2 hours

For the meringue
- 3 eggs
- 175g (6oz) caster sugar
- a pinch of salt

For the filling
- 150ml (5fl oz) double cream, whipped (optional)
- 1 nectarine
- 1 mango
- 1 kiwi

Equipment
- baking sheet
- baking parchment
- large bowl
- electric whisk
- tablespoon

- metal mixing spoon
- piping bag
- oven gloves
- chopping board
- sharp knife
- large mixing bowl

1

Line a baking sheet with baking parchment and ask an adult to preheat the oven to 110°C (225°F/Gas ¼). Separate the egg whites from the yolks.

2

Whisk the egg whites and salt in a large bowl (using an electric whisk is easier), until they form stiff peaks.

Berry-tastic

You can put any type of fruit into the meringue's centre. Try a berry medley of blueberries, raspberries and strawberries.

3

When the egg whites are stiff, whisk 5 tablespoons of the measured sugar into the mixture, 1 tablespoon at a time. Then, fold the remaining sugar into the mixture, using a metal spoon.

4

Draw 3 circles of 10cm (4in) diameter (a saucer works well) onto the parchment. Using a piping bag, squeeze out the mixture in a spiral. Pipe small peaks to create a crown. Three meringues fit on a sheet.

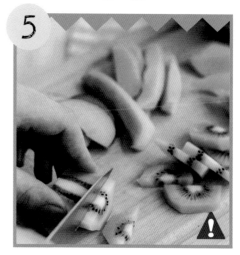

5

Towards the end of the meringue's baking time (on the bottom shelf for 2 hours), whip the cream till firm (if using) and carefully slice your fruit, and fill the centre of each crown.

Berry alternative

If blueberries aren't your fave, then you can simply use blackberries or raspberries instead. Whichever you choose, the finished result will still be a knockout.

Blueberry cheesecake

Serves 4 | 10 mins | 1 hr 20 mins

These layered desserts look impressive but are easy-peasy to make. Making them in glasses means you can see the colourful layers.

1

Place three-quarters of the berries and half of the sugar into a small saucepan. Cover and simmer for 5 minutes until soft. Stir in the other berries and leave to cool.

2

Using a clean wooden spoon, beat the cream cheese, crème fraîche, remaining sugar, and vanilla extract together in a mixing bowl. Continue until well mixed and soft.

3

Create a layered look by filling 4 glasses with a spoonful of the blueberry sauce, then a spoonful of the cream cheese mixture, and then a spoonful of the crushed biscuits.

4

Repeat the layers once more and then put the filled glasses in the refrigerator for an hour to give the mixture time to set. Serve chilled straight from the fridge.

Ingredients
- 500g (1lb 2oz) blueberries
- 2tbsp caster sugar
- 250g (9oz) cream cheese
- 200ml (7fl oz) crème fraîche
- $\frac{1}{4}$ tbsp vanilla extract
- 8 oat biscuits, crushed

Equipment
- small saucepan
- wooden spoon
- bowl
- dessert spoon
- 4 glasses

Oaty crumble

A fruit crumble is a hearty dessert that will warm you up on a cold day. Apples are used in a traditional crumble, but you could also try making it with pears and blackberries.

Preheat the oven to 180°C (350°F/Gas 4). For the topping, put the wholemeal and plain white flour into a large mixing bowl and stir together with a spoon.

Add the butter. Rub the butter and flour together with your fingertips until they look like coarse breadcrumbs. Stir in the sugar, seeds, and oats, and set aside.

To make the filling, remove the skin from the apples and cut them into quarters. Then carefully remove the core and slice the fruit into bite-sized pieces.

Put the pieces of apple into the dish. Add the blueberries and pour over the apple juice. Sprinkle the sugar over the top.

Spoon over the topping the topping in an even layer then put the dish in the oven. Cook for 35 minutes until the top is crisp and beginning to brown.

Variation

You could have this dessert in the summer. Try it with nectarines, peaches, plums, rhubarb or raspberries. They're all perfect for this dish. You can serve it with ice cream to make it summery.

Serves 6-8 · 25 mins · 35 mins

Ingredients

For the topping

· 75g (2¹/₂oz) plain white flour

· 75g (2¹/₂oz) wholemeal flour

· 75g (2¹/₂oz) unsalted butter (cut into small pieces)

· 75g (2¹/₂oz) light muscovado sugar

· 3 tbsp sunflower seeds

· 1 tbsp sesame seeds

· 3 tbsp rolled oats

For the filling

· 4 dessert apples

· 200g (7oz) blueberries, defrosted if frozen

· 4 tbsp fresh apple juice

· 1 tbsp light muscovado sugar

Equipment

· large mixing bowl

· small sharp knife

· chopping board

· 900ml (1¹/₂ pints) ovenproof dish

· small jug

PLANNING A PARTY

Pizza pops page 42

Strawberry tarts page 96

Finger foods and mini versions of your favourites work best at parties – then you don't even need cutlery. Here are some of our party faves.

A pop-up invitation

1 First, potato print some stars on to thick paper. Once they have dried, cut them out leaving a white border around the edge.

2 Fold a piece of long white card in half, and then in half again. This will make make four equal panels when you unfold the paper (as above).

3 Make two parallel cuts across the centre (see above). Wiggle your finger under this strip until it stands up from the card. Apply glue to the outer panels of the card and stick them down.

4 Stick your cut-out printed shape on to the sticking out strip. Decorate before writing your party's time and place.

Treats to take home

Decorate gingerbread shapes and pop them on sticks. Place in individual polythene bags for great party take-home treats. Yum!

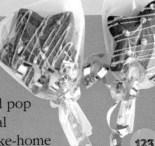

123

A THREE-COURSE MEAL

Show off your cheffing skills by cooking a meal for your friends or family. Serve up an easy feast by choosing at least two dishes that can be made in advance. And give plan out your time to make sure you and your table will be ready for your dinner guests.

Design a place card

1 Potato print your design (we chose strawberries) on to some card. Add extra details with a fine paintbrush if you like.

NOTE: The "pips" were made by making small holes in the potato.

2 Fold some thick card in half, and then add a paper panel for the name. Stick on your motif, and lastly, write on your guests' names.

Jack

The finishing touches

It's time to set the table. Alongside flowers and your handmade menu, use some pretty decorated plastic cutlery. Paint a fork with acrylic paint, and, when it's dry, tie with ribbon, and stick onto the card.

Crinkly edged paper on top looks great

Tonight
Starter
Crisp crostini with tiny tomatoes and mozzarella cheese

Main
Rigatoni pasta bolognese

Dess
Mint choc pots

Tiny tomatoes page 50

Brighten up your table with multicoloured straws and napkins.

Flowers – from the garden or florist – make a pretty addition to any table.

Mint chocolate pots page 112

Jack

Beef pasta page 56

PICNIC TIME

Never be short of ideas for eating outdoors – or even an indoor picnic if rain dampens your plans. Just pick and choose from recipes in the book.

Cupcakes page 100

Things to bring

- picnic rug
- bottles of drinks
- plates, cups, and cutlery
- paper napkins
- sunshine!

Make a paper flag

1 You'll need a pencil, some card, wooden skewers, scissors, and glue. Fold the card and draw a flag shape on the fold and cut it out.

2 Paint a design on to the flag. Cover the inside with glue, press firmly around the skewer, and leave to dry. Plant each flag proudly in your food.

Vegetable tart page 78

Potato salad page 64

Brownies
page 106

Picnic salad page 26

Hummus and veggie
sticks always go
down well.

Italian bread page 34

BBQ chicken page 74

Use the flags to identify
vegetarian recipes
perhaps, or any that
contain nuts.

127

Index